HORRIBLE HISTORIES

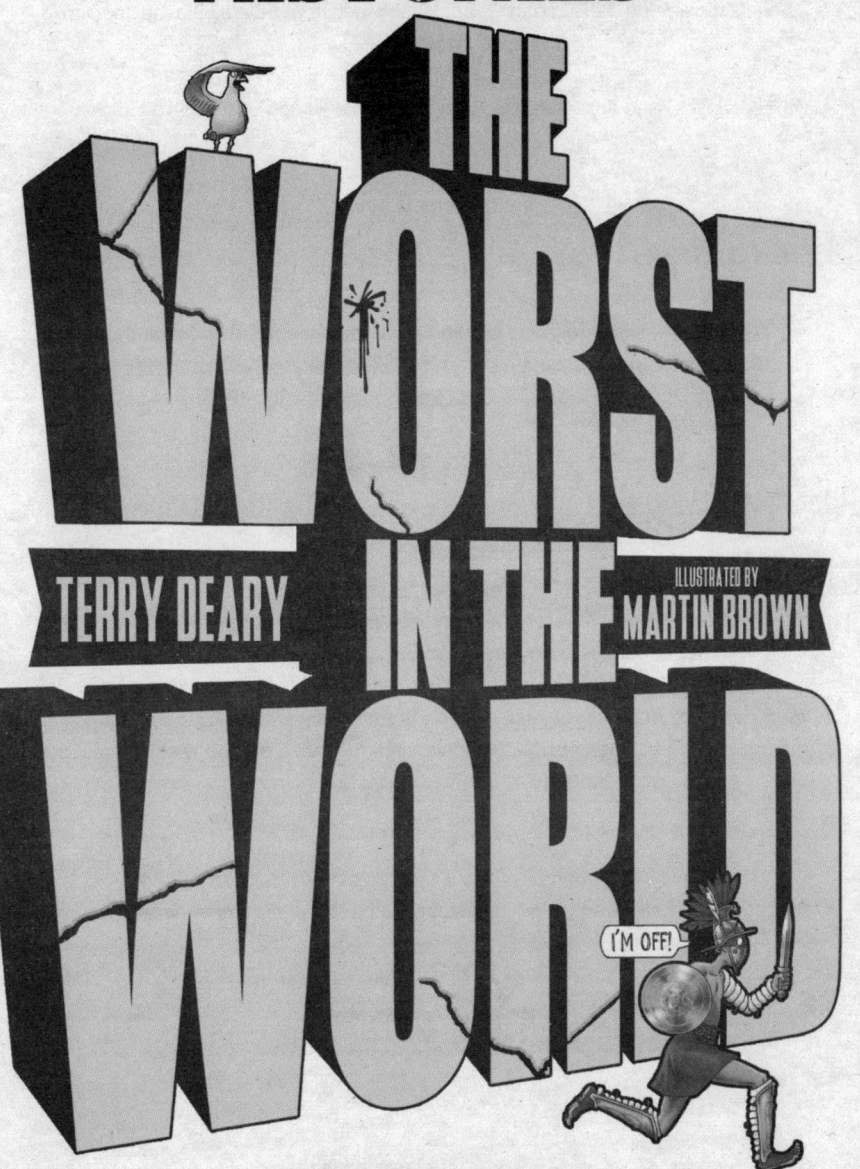

Published in the UK by Scholastic, 2023
1 London Bridge, London, SE1 9BG
Scholastic Ireland, 89E Lagan Road, Dublin Industrial Estate, Glasnevin, Dublin, D11 HP5F

SCHOLASTIC and associated logos are trademarks and/or registered trademarks of Scholastic Inc.

Text © Terry Deary, 2023
Cover illustration © Martin Brown, 2023
Text illustrations © Martin Brown, 2023

The right of Terry Deary and Martin Brown to be identified as the author and illustrator of this work respectively has been asserted by them in accordance with the Copyright, Designs and Patents Act, 1988.

ISBN 978 0702 32376 8

A CIP catalogue record for this book is available from the British Library.

All rights reserved.
This book is sold subject to the condition that it shall not, by way of trade or otherwise, be lent, hired out or otherwise circulated in any form of binding or cover other than that in which it is published. No part of this publication may be reproduced, stored in a retrieval system, or transmitted in any form or by any other means (electronic, mechanical, photocopying, recording or otherwise) without prior written permission of Scholastic Limited.

Printed and bound in Great Britain by Clays Ltd, Elcograf S.p.A
Paper made from wood grown in sustainable forests and other controlled sources.

4 6 8 10 9 7 5 3

www.scholastic.co.uk

CONTENTS

Introduction   9

The Worst Food in the World   11
Gold – Stone Age (c. 10,000 BC)   12
Silver – Roman Feasts (AD 69)   15
Bronze – French Fancies (1870)   18

The Worst Olympic Sport in the World   20
Gold – Greek Olympics (776 BC)   21
Silver – Cotswold Olympics (1612)   25
Bronze – Modern Olympics (1896)   28

The Worst Disease in the World   30
Gold – Smallpox   31
Silver – Leprosy   35
Bronze – Cholera   37

The Worst Battle in the World   40
Gold – Changping (260 BC)   41
Silver – Hastings (1066)   45
Bronze – Butchering Bosworth (1485)   48

The Worst Sea Disaster in the World   51
Gold – Carthage (255 BC)   52
Silver – SS *Eastland* (1915)   54
Bronze – Morro Castle (1934)   56

The Worst Emperor in the World   59
Gold – Zheng (221–210 BC)   60
Silver – Irene of Athens (AD 797–802)   63
Bronze – Alexander the Great (336–323 BC)   65

The Worst Rebellion in the World   68
Gold – Spartacus (73–71 BC)   69
Silver – The French Revolution (1789–99)   72
Bronze – The Haiti Slave Revolt (1791–1804)   74

The Worst Natural Disaster in the World   76
Gold – Volcano at Pompeii (AD 79)   77
Silver – Irish Famine (1845–52)   80
Bronze – Meteorite (66 million years ago)   83

The Worst Punishments in the World   85
Gold – The Roman Games (AD 80)   86
Silver – Sepoy Rebellions (1857–58)   89
Bronze – Hanged, Drawn and Quartered (1605)   92

The Worst Youths in the World — 94
Gold – Elagabalus (AD 218–222) — 95
Silver – Murad IV (1612–40) — 98
Bronze – Julius Caesar of Austria (1584–1609) — 100

The Worst Palace in the World — 102
Gold – The Tower of London — 103
Silver – Buckingham Palace — 106
Bronze – Versailles, France — 109

The Worst Knight in the World — 112
Gold – The Black Douglas (1286–1330) — 113
Silver – Simon de Montfort (1175–1218) — 116
Bronze – William de Tracy (1135–90) — 119

The Worst Pandemic in the World — 121
Gold – The Black Death (1346–53) — 122
Silver – Spanish Flu (1918–1920) — 125
Bronze – Athens Plague (430–426 BC) — 127

The Worst Religion in the World — 129
Gold – Aztec Gods (1400s) — 130
Silver – The Crusades (1097) — 133
Bronze – Ireland (1649) — 136

The Worst Cure in the World — 138
Gold – Inca (1430s) — 139
Silver – Georgians (1750s) — 142
Bronze – Plague Cures (1346–53) — 144

The Worst Enslaver in the World — 146
Gold – Christopher Columbus (1451–1506) — 147
Silver – Elizabeth I (1533–1603) — 150
Bronze – The Romans (700s BC) — 152

The Worst Women in the World — 154
Gold – Elizabeth Bathory (1560–1614) — 155
Silver – Amina, Nigerian Queen of Zazzau (1533–1610) — 158
Bronze – Lucrezia Borgia (1480–1519) — 160

The Worst Job in the World — 163
Gold – Groom of the Stool (1509–47) — 164
Silver – Mudlark (1800s) — 167
Bronze – Match Making (1880s) — 169

The Worst Journey in the World — 171
Gold – Magellan (1480–1521) — 172
Silver – James Cook (1728–79) — 176
Bronze – Captain Scott (1868–1912) — 178

The Worst Ruler in the World — 180
Gold – Ivan the Terrible (Tsar from 1547–84) — 181
Silver – Henry VIII (ruled in 1509–47) — 185
Bronze – Shaka, Zulu chief (ruled in 1816–28) — 187

The Worst Torturer in the World — 189
Gold – William Waad (1546–1623) — 190
Silver – Thomas of Torquemada (1420–98) — 193
Bronze – Matthew Hopkins (1620–47) — 195

The Worst Castle in the World — 197
Gold – Hylton Castle (1606) — 198
Silver – Leap Castle, Ireland (1250) — 201
Bronze – Moosham Castle, Austria (1675) — 203

The Worst Robber in the World — 205
Gold – Twm Siôn Cati (1530–1609) — 206
Silver – Ned Kelly (1854–80) — 209
Bronze – Carl Gugasian (1947–) — 211

The Worst War in the World — 213
Gold – The Thirty Years' War (1618–48) — 214
Silver – The First World War (1914–18) — 217
Bronze – Timur's Wars (1370–1405) — 219

The Worst Pirate in the World — 221
Gold – William Fly (died c. 1726) — 222
Silver – Blackbeard (c. 1680–1718) — 225
Bronze – Grainne (c. 1530–1603) — 227

The Worst Highway Robber in the World — 230
Gold – Dick Turpin (1705–39) — 231
Silver – Thuggees (1200–1800) — 235
Bronze – Jennie 'Little Britches' Stephens — 237

The Worst Assassination in the World — 240
Gold – Archduke Ferdinand (1863–1914) — 241
Silver – Gao Jianli (230 BC) — 244
Bronze – Hasan Sabah (1050–1124) — 246

The Worst Invasion in the World — 248
Gold – Tasmania (1802) — 249
Silver – Lindisfarne (AD 793) — 253
Bronze – The Americas (1492) — 255

The Worst School in the World — 257
Gold – Bowes Academy (1823) — 258
Silver – Birmingham Girls' School (1920) — 262
Bronze – Tudor School — 264

The Worst Weapon in the World — 266
Gold – The Atomic Bomb (1945) — 267
Silver – The Anti-Tank Dog (1940s) — 270
Bronze – The Circular Warship (1877) — 273

Epilogue — 276

Index — 278

INTRODUCTION

A sailor fell ill in the Pacific Ocean…

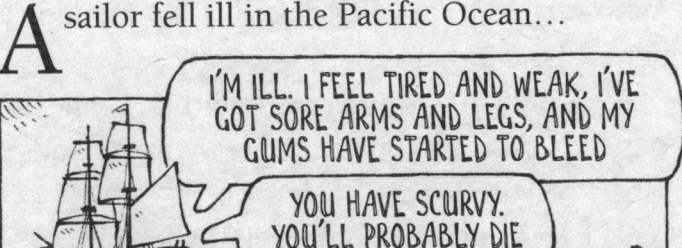

And the sailor thought…

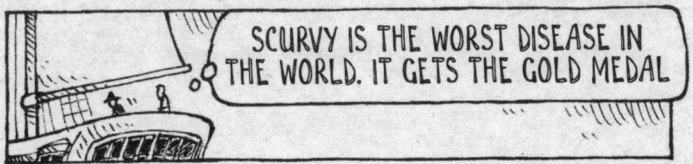

A woman in a French village in the Middle Ages fell ill…

And the woman thought…

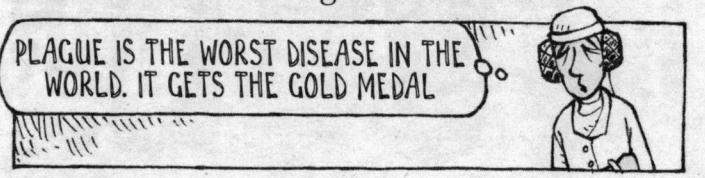

Who is right? They BOTH are. They just don't agree.

A lot of 'worst' things are like that. It all depends on who you are, where you are and when you are living (or dying).

So here are thirty gold medal-winning worsts. There are thirty silver medals for second worst and thirty bronze for third worst.

Whether or not you agree is up to you.

THE WORST FOOD IN THE WORLD

AND YOU THOUGHT SCHOOL DINNERS WERE BAD!

STONE AGE (c. 10,000 BC)

If the first humans wanted meat, they had to catch it – or find a dead animal – and gut it before they could cook it.

COOK IT? WHAT'S THAT? WE JUST BURN IT A BIT

A Stone Age recipe would look like this ... if they could write.

MEAT TREAT

1. Skin your beast with your stone knives. Cut the guts out because you won't want to picnic on poo.
2. Strike a flint to set fire to straw and then add wood.
3. Throw your dead animal on to the fire and scorch it till the meat is black and crispy on the outside.
4. Tear off the flesh and share it round the family.
5. The meat inside may be raw and bloody but don't worry, that makes it even yummier.
6. Serve it with fresh water.

If you can't catch something big and tasty then you can always eat roots and berries or nuts and seeds. If you fancy a tasty crunch then don't eat crisps, eat insects.

> LOOK MUMMY, A YUMMY DUNG BEETLE

> I'M DUNG FOR!

If you wanted something sweet, you had to rob a hive. Risky, but if you get the honey it will *bee* good for you. The bees disagree, of course.

ROMAN FEASTS (AD 69)

In Ancient Rome most people ate meat, vegetables, fruit and bread. But the rich Romans liked to show off. They ate food that was rare and expensive.

Emperor Vitellius (ruled in AD 69) was famous for eating FOUR feasts a day. At one feast his brother served him 2,000 fish and 7,000 birds. Vitellius managed to keep stuffing himself by tickling his throat with a feather till he threw up. Then he had room for more food – chew, stew, spew, repeat.

His favourite snacks were livers from pike

fish, brains from pheasants and tongues from flamingos.

Emperor Elagabalus (ruled in AD 218–222) had a feast you may have enjoyed…

EMPEROR'S EATERY

STARTERS:
Brains of 600 thrushes, cockerel crests, flamingo brains, parrot heads, camel heels, peacock tongues and ostrich brains

MAIN COURSE:
Roast pig from which will fly live thrushes

SWEET TREAT:
African snails

Emperor Nero (ruled in AD 54–68) liked watching other people eat. He kept a 'glutton' – an enslaved Egyptian who had to eat anything and everything he was fed (until he became monstrously large). Best of all Nero enjoyed watching his glutton kill a human and eat him.

But beware. Don't call an emperor 'fat'. Tiberius (ruled in AD 14–37) once feasted for two whole days and two whole nights. When a poet called the emperor 'fat', Tiberius had him thrown off a cliff to his death.

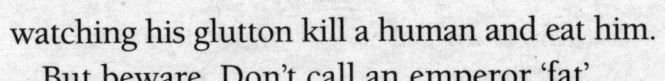

ROSES ARE RED,
VIOLETS ARE BLUE,
THE FAT BLOKE HE
THREW ME,
TO SEE IF I FLEW

FRENCH FANCIES (1870)

In 1870 the people of Paris rebelled. They called themselves 'Communards' and said...

WE WANT SO MANY PUBLIC TOILETS IN PARIS THAT NO ONE WILL EVER HAVE TO PEE IN THE STREETS AGAIN.

When a German army surrounded the city, the people were trapped. They began to starve. First to go to the butchers were the city's family horses, working horses and racehorses. Then the starving people of Paris started on the cats and dogs and rats.

One man wrote...

When you boil a cat up with nuts and olives it makes a very dainty dish.

In the end they went to Paris Zoo and killed the deer, followed by the camels, kangaroos, wolves and zebras. The monkeys were kept alive.

THE PEOPLE THOUGHT THEY WERE TOO MUCH LIKE HUMANS

THE CITY'S DIRE PREDICAMENT NOTWITHSTANDING, I CONSIDER THAT RATHER ELEMENTARY COMPARISON BOTH PATRONIZING AND MORE THAN A LITTLE IMPERTINENT

In the end they shot two elephants and sold the meat. Only the very rich could afford it.

One jumbo-eater said...

IT IS TOUGH AND OILY. STICK TO BEEF

SORRY

THE WORST OLYMPIC SPORT IN THE WORLD

FASTER, HIGHER, DEADER

GREEK OLYMPICS (776 BC)

Once humans had learned to farm for food, they didn't have to spend all their time hunting. They had time for 'sport'. The Ancient Greeks decided to see who was best in the land. They invented the Olympic Games – because they took place near Mount Olympus.

Only men took part back in 776 BC. The men raced with no clothes on, and women were not allowed to even watch.

But some of the 'games' turned savage. One form of wrestling was called 'pankration'. It was a bit of a mixture of boxing and wrestling. The only rule was there were no rules apart from no biting and no gouging out the eyes. Just flatten your opponent. You could…

- Strangle
- Kick
- Arm-twist
- Jump up and down on them

Pankration could be deadly.

THE GREEK GUARDIAN
STILL ONLY 20 OBOLS

CREUGAS THE CORPSE CLAIMS CROWN

In the Olympic pankration event, Damoxenos, the champ, beat challenger Creugas … and also lost the title. A crowd of 2,000 sat on the grass to enjoy a fight to the end. They didn't know what an end it was going to be.

BOOS

Big Damoxenos was booed as he stepped on to the grass and had leather wrapped around his mighty fists. The handsome Creugas was cheered as he stepped forward.

The referee stepped back. 'Box!' he cried and Damoxenos lunged forward. He swung his fist like a mighty hammer at Creugas, but the young man jumped back and flicked a punch at the champ's head.

That was how the fight went on ... and on. Big Damoxenos lumbering round, swinging huge punches but unable to catch the slippery Creugas. The sun began to sink down and the referee called a halt.

'We cannot have a draw,' he cried. 'The contest will be decided by a single blow struck by each man.'

FIRST

'You go first, wimp,' Damoxenos growled. The big man held his arms by his side – the crowd held its breath. Creugas struck a hammer blow to the champion's head. The big man just laughed. 'My turn.'

Instead of punching, the big ox hit Creugas cruelly under the ribs with straight fingers. His sharp fingernails tore through the young man's skin.

Damoxenos pulled back his hand and jabbed again. This time he tore out the challenger's guts.

The crowd gasped as Creugas fell lifeless to the ground. The ref ran forward. 'One blow is all that is allowed. You took two blows, Damoxenos, you cheat. I hereby disqualify you. I declare Creugas the champion.' The crowd cheered. Creugas the corpse was too dead to hear the cheer.

Creugas will always be remembered as a champion who had guts.

COTSWOLD OLYMPICS (1612)

The Romans banned the Olympics and the games vanished for 1,500 years. The modern Olympics were started again in 1896 by Pierre de Coubertin, a young French nobleman. Since then, they have been staged every fourth year.

BUT everyone (except *Horrible Histories*) forgets the 'Cotswold Olimpicks' that were held near Stratford-upon-Avon in the days of the great writer William Shakespeare who lived there.

They began in 1612 and went on until the Games ended in the 1850s. But some sports like SHIN-KICKING went on in other places.

There is now a World Shin-Kicking Championship. Crowds of thousands of people turn up to watch. If you want rules...

SHIN-KICKING RULES

- Fighters must be over eighteen.
- They must face each other and hold on to each other's collar.
- The fight begins when the referee tosses a coin.
- The winner gets first kick.
- The aim is to strike their opponent's shin with the inside of the foot as well as their toes.
- The first to cry out 'enough' is the loser.

Stories say some of the first shin-kickers wore steel-toed boots. They trained their legs to take the pain by hitting their shins with hammers. Some fighters ended up maimed for life, while some even died from their injuries.

Welsh fighters wore thick shoes with nails sticking out the sides. Nowadays the fighters must wear soft shoes and they stuff their trouser legs with straw.

MODERN OLYMPICS (1896)

When the modern Olympics began again in 1896 there were some odd games we wouldn't see today.

- Swimming obstacle race (1900)
- Tug of war (1900 to 1920)
- Rope climb (1896 to 1932 ... and in 1904 won by a man with one wooden leg)
- Duelling pistols (1896 to 1912 ... using wax bullets)

But the bronze medal for the world's worst Olympic sport goes to live pigeon shooting.

The 1900 Games was the only time when animals were killed for sport during a modern Olympics. Over 300 pigeons were killed in those Games. The gold was won by a Belgian named Léon de Lunden, who had twenty-one kills.

Even in those days a lot of people found it sick, and it was replaced with clay pigeon shooting.

THE WORST DISEASE IN THE WORLD

I'M SICK TO DEATH OF THIS

SMALLPOX

....

The thing about smallpox is it didn't matter who you were, it could strike you down. From measly monarch to spotty slave, they could all suffer. A doctor would tell you…

HHS Horrible Health Service

SMALLPOX

Smallpox is caused by a virus and has been around for thousands of years. You catch it by coming into close contact with infected people, if you breathe in their droplets of spit and snot.

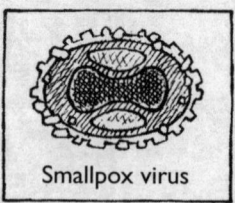
Smallpox virus

The virus grows inside you quietly for ten to fourteen days before you feel a bit fluey. Then spots appear all over, you feel very ill and you take to your bed.

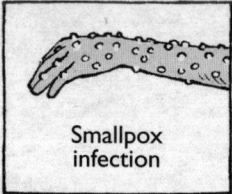
Smallpox infection

Over the next few days, the spots begin to ooze fluid over your skin. After suffering for about fourteen days you may die. Well, about one in every three people do.

The earliest known victim was a pharaoh – a king of Egypt. The mummy of Ramses V (ruled in 1145–1140 BC) has been unwrapped and shows his skin is scarred with a disease that looks a lot like smallpox. He must have been annoyed with his doctor. What a spot of bother!

PHYSICIANS TO THE PHARAOHS

Feeling frail? Pay us to keep you perky.

THAT'S OUR MUMMY-BACK GUARANTEE.

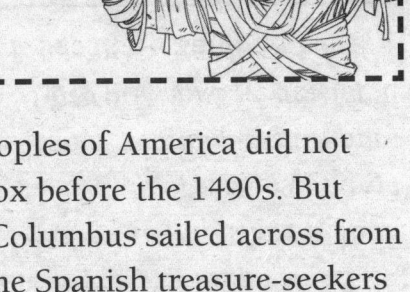

The indigenous peoples of America did not suffer from smallpox before the 1490s. But then Christopher Columbus sailed across from Europe in 1492. The Spanish treasure-seekers followed him and took slaves and gold. In return they left behind European diseases.

The indigenous Haitians numbered around a million. When Columbus and his successors landed. By the 1560s, during the reign of Elizabeth I, there was not one Haitian left – one million to zero in seventy years – wiped out by diseases like smallpox and influenza.

In 1562, Elizabeth I fell ill with smallpox. Panic in England: there was no heir ready to take the throne. She recovered though.

There was a story that a noblewoman from Elizabeth's court took to wearing a mask to hide her smallpox-scarred face. Mary Sidney came down with smallpox while serving the queen. Her husband, Sir Henry, described her suffering...

> When I went to Newhaven, I left her a full fair lady, and when I returned I found her as foul a lady as the smallpox could make her. The scars ever since remain on her face, so as she lives like a night raven in her house.

GEE, THANKS FOR YOUR SUPPORT, DARLING

Mary caught the disease from nursing Elizabeth in 1562. How did Elizabeth reward such a faithful servant? She gave her...

a) Her weight in gold
b) A mask covered in jewels to hide the scars
c) The sack

Answer: (c) Elizabeth 'rewarded' Mary with the sack. What else did you expect? Mary and her husband lost all their money and died poor.

LEPROSY

Leprosy is as old as smallpox, and people caught it by being close to anyone who suffered from the disease.

So, the answer was to send the lepers away to live alone in a 'colony'. This still happens in parts of India, Africa and China. If a leper DID go into a town, they had to wear a cloth across their mouth and cry:

'Unclean, unclean.'

An ancient story from 700 BC in Sri Lanka says...

Princess Priya and King Rawma caught the disease. They had to live in the wilderness until they were cured with the help of herbs.

Your muscles feel weak, and you lose the feeling in some places. If you can't feel your fingers, you feel no pain if you damage them.

The writers of the Bible said leprosy was a punishment from God. If you rebel, then catching leprosy is what happens to you and only God can cure you.

FOR HEAVEN'S SAKE...

Go to your local temple now. The priests can cure ANY disease with their prayers.

Simply give them all your money... or there'll be hell to pay.

CHOLERA

I n Victorian times cholera brought terror to thousands.

January 1848

GO BLUE AND DIE

The people of London are in a panic as cholera kills thousands. Our readers are asking, 'What is this dreadful disease? And how do we know if we have it?'

Cholera is a devilish little germ that lives in your guts. It kills most of the people who catch it. Your poo turns to water and pours out of your bottom. At the other end you keep vomiting. Your skin turns blue and then you die ... if you don't get treated.

Henry Mayhew, a health inspector, was shocked to see the way the poor people of London got their water. He wrote...

As we gazed in horror, we saw a little child lower a tin can with a rope into a ditch to fill a large bucket that stood beside her. The people left the mucky liquid to stand. After it has rested for a day or two, they skim the filth off the top and use it to cook and drink and wash. We went to a house where a baby lay dead of the cholera. We asked if they really did drink the water. The answer was, 'Yes, we have to drink from the ditch, unless we can beg or steal a pail of water.'

DID YOU KNOW...?

So many Londoners died of cholera in the 1849 outbreak that the graveyards filled up. They had to build a special burial ground in the countryside. Corpses were carried there by train and had their own station built next to Waterloo Station. Local people said...

THE WORST BATTLE IN THE WORLD

DON'T LOSE YOUR HEAD

CHANGPING (260 BC)

The world's worst battle went on for two YEARS. In the 300s BC China was split into large states who all wanted to rule the whole country. They just had to fight one another.

It was a bit like a football cup competition. The small teams (or states) were knocked out until there were just two big states left to battle out the final.

In the west were the Qin (pronounced 'chin'). Nobody liked the Qin. They were rough horse-riding people. They had simple music. One lord from East China was very snobby. He said…

The other big state in the cup final was Zhao. Qin attacked Zhao. But Zhao built a strong line of trenches at Changping. There was no getting through Zhao.

They went on attacking and defending for two years. It was no win for the Qin … until they had a clever idea. And it wasn't about attacking. They started telling stories to the rest of China about the Zhao.

At last, the Zhao emperor got to hear the stories.

The new Zhao general attacked the Qin, who ran away … or pretended to. When the Zhao had left their safe trenches, the Qin turned and made a circle around their enemy.

The Zhao general gave up and the Zhao laid down their weapons. It made no difference. The Qin army killed every single enemy soldier. Half a million Zhao died, and the Qin ruled China.

DID YOU KNOW...?

Emperor Xuanzong of Tang (ruled in AD 712–756) collected some of the bones from that great battle at Changping. He built a temple over some of the human remains and buried the rest of them in mass graves. Today, 2,300 years later, people are still finding bones.

HASTINGS (1066)

Pretending to run away is a trick that's been used in many battles in history – but the generals (who never read *Horrible Histories*) never learn.

In 1066, William, the duke of Normandy (then king of England until 1087), invaded England to claim the English crown from his enemy, Harold. William landed at Hastings and marched to meet King Harold's army, who were sitting safely on top of a hill.

The Norman soldiers were afraid to attack up the hill. There is a legend (it may even be true) that a Norman jester led William's troops into the Battle of Hastings. The Norman historian Wace said…

A MINSTREL NAMED TAILLEFER WENT IN FRONT OF THE NORMAN ARMY, SINGING AND JUGGLING WITH HIS SWORDS WHILE THE TROOPS MARCHED BEHIND SINGING.

Sounds a bit like a bunch of football supporters on their way to a match. Taillefer began to juggle with his swords and put on a brave show. The Norman soldiers were ashamed to see a jester take the lead when they were acting like cowards. They attacked.

And what happened to Taillefer the juggling jester?

a) William made him a knight.
b) The Saxons attacked him and cut him to pieces.
c) He dropped his sword, cut his leg off and died.

Answer: (b) Yes, he was cut down by the Saxons. A lot of heroes ended up dead in history.

William of Normandy still couldn't get Harold's English troops off the hilltop. So, he tried the old trick and pretended to run away. Did it work? Of course. The Saxons charged down and were wiped out.

Harold had NOT read his *Horrible Histories* books at school, had he? William went on to be William the Conqueror. World's worst battle for the English.

WILLIAM THE CONQUEROR SOUNDS BETTER THAN WILLIAM THE TRICKY

BUTCHERING BOSWORTH (1485)

In 1485, King Richard III ruled England. But the Welsh lord Henry Tudor (1457–1509) said the throne should be his, and his army met Richard's at Bosworth Field.

Richard sat on his white war horse on top of the hill. He must have been taught how to fight a battle – he had won lots. Maybe he went to knight school?

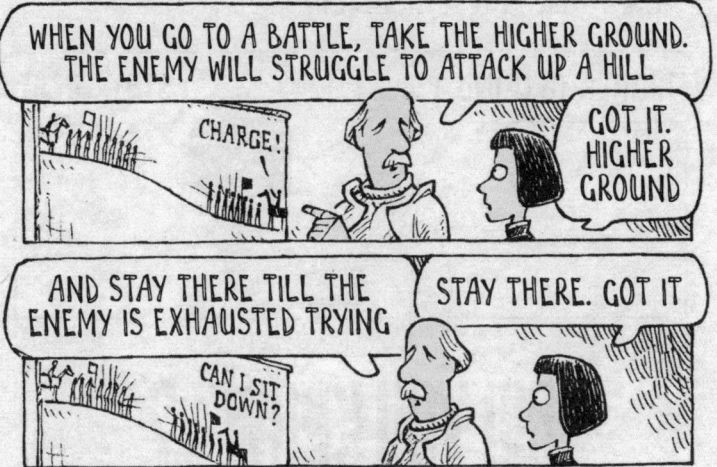

At Bosworth, Richard took the higher ground at Ambion Hill. His men fought on the lower slopes but were not doing very well. Richard decided to end the fight quickly by killing the enemy commander, Henry Tudor. He rode down off the top of the hill.

This would be the last great charge of knights in English history. His teacher must have been weeping. What happened to 'stay there'? For-got it?

Of course, Richard didn't get past Henry Tudor's bodyguards. He was cut down and killed. Henry, the first of the Terrible Tudors, took over. When you go into your next battle what must you remember?

DID YOU KNOW...?

Richard III's body was buried secretly in a monastery in Leicester. It was discovered in 2012 and buried in Leicester Cathedral. This time we hope he'll do what he should have done at Bosworth:

'Stay there.'

THE WORST SEA DISASTER IN THE WORLD

I'VE GOT THAT SINKING FEELING

CARTHAGE (255 BC)

The Romans were worse than most empires at bringing disaster to other people. But sometimes they suffered their own disasters.

The state of Carthage sat on the south side of the Mediterranean Sea – what we now call North Africa. The Roman state sat on the other side – now Italy. Two big dogs of war had to fight to see who the top dog would be. These were the Punic Wars. (Rome was the winning wolfhound in the end.)

The Romans landed in Carthage, but they couldn't take the city. They sat there.

And sat there. But then the people of Carthage paid some soldiers from Greece to attack the Romans. The Greeks brought their war elephants to help with the task ... or the tusk.

The Romans were thumped and thrashed and thwarted. The ones that were left filled hundreds of ships and sailed back to Rome. At least, that was the plan. A storm in the Mediterranean sank 284 of them and 100,000 Romans died.

It was one of the worst sea disasters in history.

BACK BAP IN BAP YOUR BAP BOATS BAP!

SS *EASTLAND* (1915)

When people think of sea disasters they think of RMS *Titanic* – unsinkable till the unthinkable happened. It hit an iceberg and sank in 1912.

THE PERFECT PRESENT: A MODEL OF THE *TITANIC*

Only £50 from all good toyshops.

Warning: not for use in the bath. Only the sink.

The world was shocked because the *Titanic* didn't have enough lifeboats. So, a new law – the Seamen's Act – said new ships must have places for everyone in the ship's life boats.

Three years later, the SS *Eastland* sat in a dock at Chicago in just six metres of water. No icebergs or Atlantic storms in sight.

Over 2,500 passengers were off to a picnic and went on the top deck to wave goodbye. Their weight made the ship lean over into the dirty water of the river.

In less than two minutes the ship was on its side, the passengers trapped or thrown into the water and drowned. Over 840 people died.

Why was the ship top heavy? Because it was carrying TOO MANY lifeboats on top, thanks to the Seamen's Act. The *Titanic* is still famous, while the *Eastland*, sunk by the *Titanic* law, is forgotten.

SS *MORRO CASTLE* (1934)

On the *Titanic* many of the passengers and crew behaved with calm and courage, giving up their place in the lifeboats to someone else. But a fire on the cruise ship SS *Morro Castle* in 1934 showed the nastier side of human nature.

Dear Mother,

I am alive. I know you will be worried when you get news of the Morro Castle disaster as you know I sailed on her. It was fine until the captain had stomach pains and died – there is a story that he was poisoned.

The chief officer took command and was faced with the problem of a small fire in the passenger library. No one was worried because the owners said the Morro Castle was fireproof.

So, the ship went on at full speed over the North Atlantic towards New York and, of course, that speed whipped the flames through the decks. It was 3 a.m. and most of us passengers were asleep – no alarm was sounded to warn us.

Some of us smelled the smoke and staggered onto the deck to climb into lifeboats. Others simply jumped overboard without waiting for a boat.

They say 134 of the 549 people aboard died. The ship drifted to the shore, and I was rowed in a lifeboat on to the beach. I am well, Mother, but sick with disgust. People of America have rushed to the coast to see the wreck, but that wreck is the graveyard of all those poor people, burned alive. Some evil showmen have claimed the best spaces on the rocks. They are selling tickets to the ghouls who want to go and stare. Humans can be horrible.

Your loving son,
John

THE WORST EMPEROR IN THE WORLD

IT'S TOUGH AT THE TOP

ZHENG (221–210 BC)

Many rulers in history have been cruel. A lot have been unthinking. Most have been both. And many have been led into cruelty by 'advisers' or ministers.

Ying Zheng became lord of all of China in 221 BC (ruled as Emperor of Qin in 235–221 BC and King of Qin in 221–210 BC) and called himself Shi Huangdi – meaning 'The First Great Emperor'. Other emperors in history have killed millions of enemies. Zheng caused a million of his own people to die.

Zheng's prime minister was the ruthless

and cunning Li Si. Sometimes clever people came to Zheng and told him he couldn't make a change because the law books said he couldn't. Li Si had the perfect answer.

BURN THE BOOKS. SORTED.

> **HORRIBLE HISTORIES note:**
> If you have paid for this book then you can burn it to keep your granny warm in winter.

Up in North China there were travelling bands of warriors raiding the country. Zheng built walls across the passes the enemy rode through. The warriors could climb those walls with ladders, of course. But their horses couldn't.

The walls were a great idea, but it took soldiers and peasants to build them. Well over a million of Zheng's people died from the effort. A legend said…

Zheng took a medicine made with mercury to let him live for ever. In fact, it probably poisoned him. Prime Minister Li Si was worried that the lords would go to war to replace Zheng. He kept the emperor's corpse behind a curtain and pretended Zheng could still speak and take orders from him.

When Zheng's body began to smell Li Si had a load of rotten fish brought to the palace to hide the Zheng pong.

IRENE OF ATHENS
(AD 797–802)

How far would you go to take the emperor's throne?

Irene (ruled in AD 797–802) was married to Roman Emperor Leo IV from 775 to 780. When he died, their son Constantine VI took the throne, but he was only nine years old. So, his kind mummy Irene ruled for him.

But when Constantine VI grew older, he wanted to replace her. What could she do? What would YOU do, Irene?

a) Retire to a bungalow by the seaside
b) Kill yourself because you lost the throne
c) Have Constantine VI's eyes put out and lock him away to die

The answer is (c), of course (because this is a *Horrible Histories* book). Irene got her friends to blind her own son.

ALEXANDER THE GREAT
(RULED IN 336–23 BC)

Killing your son is bad, Irene. But killing your dad's as bad. That's what Alexander the Great did to his father, Philip II of Macedon, northeastern Greece.

THE MACEDON MAIL

PHILIP II ASSASSINATED

Reports are coming in that our dear King Philip has been murdered in the street.

Philip was going to the theatre. He wanted to show his Greek guests just how popular with the people he was.

The attack, when it came, was by his own bodyguard, Pausanias of Orestis. The assassin tried to escape and reach his friends who were waiting for him with horses. He was chased by three of Philip's bodyguards but tripped on a vine root and was speared by his pursuers. He was, of course, unable to explain who ordered the assassination. But *The Macedon Mail* points the finger of blame at Alexander.

Alexander the Murdering Brat became Alexander the Great as he marched across Asia, killing a quarter of a million enemy soldiers. But add on another quarter of a million innocent people.

Awesome Alex took the throne at twenty years old and swept through the Middle East and Egypt to India. Then he moaned...

His army rebelled, so he marched them back home … the hard way. So hard, more than half of them died. Then Alex died from drinking too much wine … Alexander the Grape?

Or was he poisoned? Some people would say it served him right.

THE WORST REBELLION IN THE WORLD

SPARTACUS (73–71 BC)

Alexander's soldiers rebelled because they were marched halfway across the world. But when the millions of poor get organized, they can rebel to put an end to their awful lives.

In Rome the rebellion came from the slaves who had to work to let the rich Romans live a comfy life. In 73 BC a gladiator called Spartacus led a rebellion in the south of Italy against the Romans.

Who was he? He was from Thrace (it's called Bulgaria on maps now) and he joined the Roman army. Then he deserted and became an outlaw. When he was captured, he was forced to fight as a gladiator. He was so good he became a gladiator teacher.

Then he decided to go home and lead all his gladiator friends to freedom. A Greek writer Plutarch wrote...

> And now Spartacus was joined by farmers and shepherds of those parts, all tough men and fast on their feet. Some of these were armed as soldiers and some were used as spies.

Spartacus had a real army now, not just a bunch of bandits. The Roman army chased Spartacus, but the gladiator won the battles. He made the Roman prisoners fight to the death. It was his way of taking revenge.

But in the end Spartacus's slave army couldn't beat General Crassus and his huge Roman army – it took eight legions (about 50,000 men) to beat the rebels. Six thousand of Spartacus's rebels were captured and crucified. Crassus placed the crosses at the sides of the main road into Rome as a lesson.

Crassus did not give orders for the bodies to be taken down. Slaves walking along the road were forced to see the bodies for years after the last battle. It was a warning. No one knows if Spartacus was killed in the final battle or if he was caught alive and executed.

THE FRENCH REVOLUTION (1789–99)

In the 1780s the French peasants were starving. An Englishman, Arthur Young, visited France and was shocked…

> Many of the ploughmen and their wives have no shoes or stockings. The children look hungry. Their clothes are so ragged they may as well not have any. I saw one little girl whose only toy was a stick. It made my heart ache to see her.

The English writer Tobias Smollett described the peasants a few years earlier...

They are more like starved scarecrows than human beings.

The peasants turned against their noble lords and ladies and sent them to the chopping machine known as the guillotine. In 1793 King Louis XVI was chopped along with his wife, Marie Antoinette.

Over 16,000 people were guillotined in the revolution, most of them in the nine months between autumn 1793 and summer 1794. Many more people were shot or died of sickness in the prisons. The revolution cost over 50,000 lives.

THE HAITI REVOLT (1791–1804)

As the peasants revolted in France, the enslaved in the French colony of Haiti got the idea. In 1791 the people enslaved in the north of the island rebelled and slaughtered around 2,000 of their French and British colonizers.

They burned down the coffee and sugar plantations where they'd been forced to work. The bosses brought in troops and massacred 10,000 people.

The French army leader, Charles Leclerc, said

he would make peace. In 1802 he agreed to let the enslaved leader, Toussaint L'Ouverture, be the leader of free Haiti. He even invited Toussaint to a dinner party to celebrate.

Toussaint was shipped back to France, shut in a dungeon, and died of cold and hunger within a year.

In 1803 the French gave up trying to crush the enslaved people of Haiti. But by then 400,000 people from Haiti and Europe had died.

What finished the French? Yellow fever. It even killed Leclerc … which sort of served him right.

THE WORST NATURAL DISASTER IN THE WORLD

IT'LL MAKE YOU SHAKE!

VOLCANO ERUPTION AT POMPEII (AD 79)

On 20 August AD 79 small earthquakes began to shake the Roman town of Pompeii and grew stronger each day. The festival of Vulcan, the god of fires AND volcanoes, followed soon after on 23 August. Maybe someone upset Vulcan.

On 24 August the volcano Vesuvius erupted. A twenty-two-kilometre plume of smoke rose into the air. The locals watched it and suffered the ash-fall. Unpleasant? Yes. Dangerous? Nah.

They were wrong. A wave of enormous

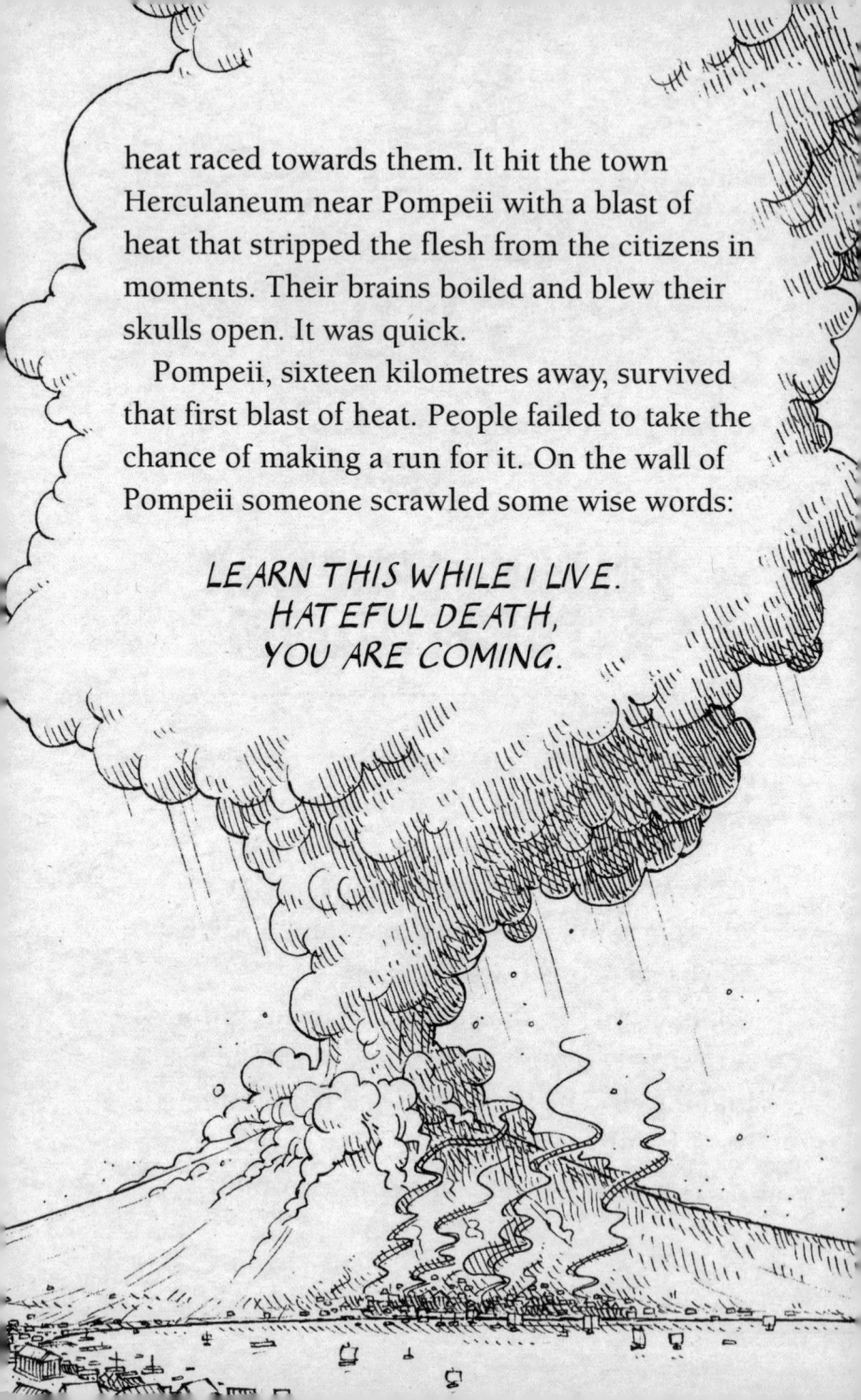

heat raced towards them. It hit the town Herculaneum near Pompeii with a blast of heat that stripped the flesh from the citizens in moments. Their brains boiled and blew their skulls open. It was quick.

Pompeii, sixteen kilometres away, survived that first blast of heat. People failed to take the chance of making a run for it. On the wall of Pompeii someone scrawled some wise words:

> LEARN THIS WHILE I LIVE.
> HATEFUL DEATH,
> YOU ARE COMING.

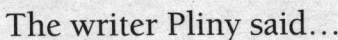

The writer Pliny said…

> You could hear the shrieks of women, the wailing of infants and the shouting of men; some were calling for their parents, others their children or their wives, trying to find them by their voices.
>
> Many cried for the gods to help, but others said there were no gods left, and that the world had been plunged into darkness for evermore.

Another wall scribbler wrote…

ONCE YOU ARE DEAD, YOU ARE NOTHING.

That's not true. Once you are dead in Pompeii, tourists will come to gawp at your ash-covered corpse for thousands of years.

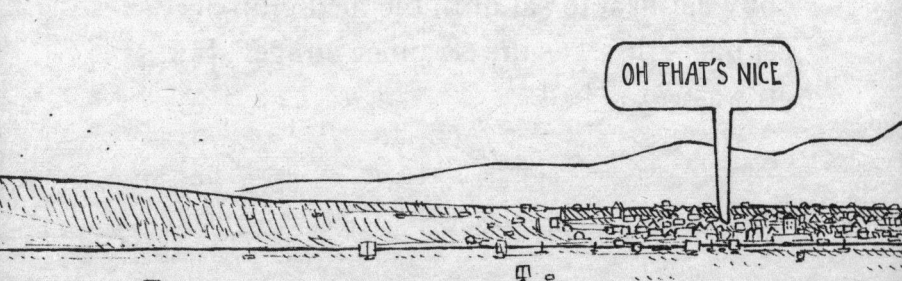

OH THAT'S NICE

IRISH FAMINE (1845–52)

Sometimes nature hits you with a disaster that means a slow death. Like death by famine.

The good news for Victorian peasants in Ireland was that potatoes grew well in their fields. You just planted your potatoes in April and May, picked them in August, then they could be stored and eaten until the following May. During summer your family had to buy oatmeal to eat until the next crop of spuds – this was the 'summer hunger', but it wasn't too bad.

With the help of this super spud the number of people in Ireland rose from 4.5 million in 1800 to 8 million in 1845. That was the good news.

But the bad news was … in August 1845 a fungus attacked the potatoes and it spread quickly over the country. The potato plants looked all right, but when you pulled them up, they were black and rotten inside.

People went hungry and began to starve to death. Asenath Nicholson – an American visitor – wrote:

> I was told of a cabin where in a dark corner a family of father, mother and two children was lying together. The father was considerably rotted, whilst the mother had died last and had fastened the door so that their bodies would not be seen. Such family scenes were quite common. The cabin was simply pulled down over the corpses as a grave.

Desperate people would eat anything...

Sure, we ate the dogs first, then the donkeys, the horses, foxes, badgers, hedgehogs and even frogs. We stewed nettles and dandelions and collected all the nuts and berries we could find. The people on the coast could eat shellfish but a lot of them were poisonous. Maybe it was better a quick death from poisoning than a slow one from hunger.

Apart from the hunger there was sickness...

> **Doctors Report:** Typhus, or Black Fever, was spread by fleas. The disease made the face swell and turn black; the victims vomited blood and they stank. When they died the fleas would find new living victims and so it spread. It became common to leave a dead family in their cabin and simply set fire to it.

Fever killed ten times as many people as hunger.

METEORITE
(66 MILLION YEARS AGO)

Are there any GOOD disasters? Look over your shoulder. Do you see a Tyrannosaurus rex about to chew you up for lunch? No. Why not? Because they are extinct.

An asteroid from space hit Earth near Mexico. It was about thirteen kilometres wide and released deadly gases as well as dust that blocked out the sun. The world turned colder. Massive waves swamped the land. Plants and about three-quarters of the animals died.

Some mammals survived and eventually evolved into humans. You (and a few billion other humans) are alive today because the dinosaurs are sleeping. Dino-snores, you could say.

A GOOD disaster.

THE WORST PUNISHMENT IN THE WORLD

EVEN WORSE THAN DETENTION

THE ROMAN GAMES
(AD 80)

Games are for fun, right? Not the Roman 'Games'. They were all about the slaughter of humans and animals. The evil emperors built arenas so their people could watch gladiators fight – often to the death. They were also places of punishment. Criminals were sent there to be executed while 50,000 Romans watched and cheered or jeered.

WE'LL HAVE TO MOVE ALL THE DEAD ANIMALS OUT FIRST

The greatest arena was the Colosseum of Rome, opened in AD 80. Animals were sent there to be hunted to death. Wild animals were often sent to tear humans apart under the baking sun.

The emperors liked to see creatures from around the Roman world. Lions, tigers, wolves, bears, leopards, wild boars, elephants, hyenas, buffalos, hippopotamuses, crocodiles, and giraffes were all seen in the Colosseum. Even rabbits.

The story of Vibia Perpetua (AD 182–203) is not a pretty one. Perpetua was a rich North African woman, and a Christian. Being Christian was a crime in Rome so she ended up in the Colosseum. Her death was awful.

For the young woman, the emperor had prepared a mad, horned cow. First the cow tossed Perpetua and she fell on her back. She asked for a pin to fasten her untidy hair.

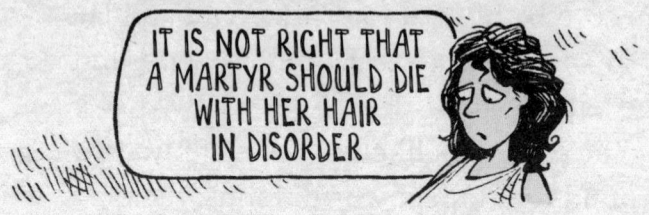

If you were facing a wild cow would your last request be 'pass the hair gel'?

A second attack left her dying and she was thrown into a corner, where it was the job of a gladiator to cut the throats of any prisoner who was not quite dead. The Roman crowd screamed for the young woman to be dragged to the centre of the arena so they could have a better view.

The young gladiator who was given the job was a bit shaky. He missed Perpetua's throat and stuck the knife into her neck. Perpetua cried out in pain, then she took the blade and guided it to her throat. At last, her suffering was over.

She was just one of 400,000 people, and maybe a million animals, who died there.

SEPOY REBELLIONS (1857–58)

Most rebellions could be avoided if the leaders would only try to understand the problems of the peasants. It's dreadful when your leader doesn't listen.

Queen Victoria's British army were really bad listeners. Around 14,000 British troops ruled 150 million people in India. The Brits had the help of almost 300,000 Indian soldiers in running the country. But the Brits were so stupid that they upset the people they should have been working with – the Indian soldiers, known as sepoys.

In 1857 it ended horribly…

But Carmichael-Smythe did. And so, the Indian Rebellion started – fourteen months of bitter fighting and dreadful slaughter. The Indians who were captured suffered a dreadful new punishment.

They were tied to the mouth of a loaded cannon. The cannon was fired and ... you can guess what happened next. The wives of the British officers watched and laughed as their dresses were spattered with the blood and guts of rebels.

But the rebellion wasn't caused by the fat bullets – it was caused by the fat heads who commanded the British army.

HANGED, DRAWN AND QUARTERED (1605)

An old English rhyme says...

Remember, remember,
the fifth of November,
Gunpowder, treason
and plot.
I see no reason, why
gunpowder treason,
Should ever be forgot.

The gunpowder plotters of this poem set out to blow up the English parliament on 5 November 1605. They were sentenced to be hanged, drawn and quartered.

Their gunpowder expert was Guy Fawkes. Guy was to die in that way … hanged by the neck until half dead. He would climb up a ladder with a rope around his neck and the ladder would be slowly taken away. Before he was dead, he would be taken down and laid on a table, where he'd have his insides cut out. Those guts would often be thrown on to a fire to burn.

Finally, he'd be beheaded and cut into four pieces. This was the punishment for 'treason', a crime against the king.

In fact, as Guy Fawkes stepped up the ladders for the hanging, he jumped so he died quickly and cleanly.

THE WORST YOUTHS IN THE WORLD

NOT YOU(TH)

ELAGABALUS (AD 218–222)

Some people just seem to be born nasty. A lot of them grew up to be Roman Emperors.

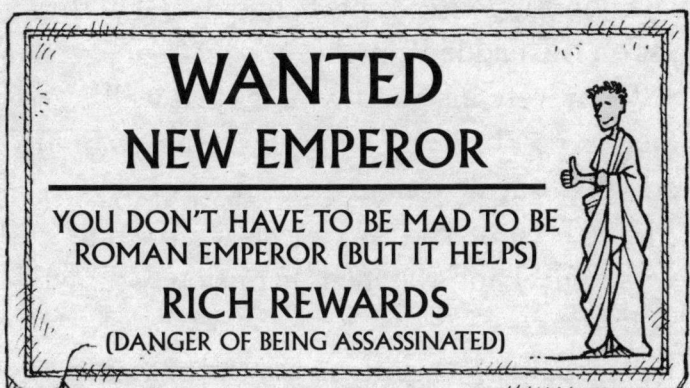

Elagabalus was priest to the sun god and was just fourteen when he was made emperor.
- He kept wearing priestly robes and leading dances around the altar.
- Romans were forced to worship at his statue. Dozens of sheep and goats were slaughtered as sacrifices.
- Mixed with their sacrificial guts were said to be the guts of young boys – Elagabalus selected only those who had both parents still alive, to watch them suffer when they were forced to watch their son's guts being spilled.
- A lion, a monkey and a snake were locked in the temple of Elagabalus and fed on bits of his enemies.
- He invented an early form of whoopee cushion for guests at his banquets when they sat on the padded couches.
- If you were his guest, you feasted well … so long as you liked camel heels, flamingo brains and nightingale tongues. But it was risky.
At one feast he had two guests strapped to a waterwheel and watched them slowly drown as it turned.
- Elagabalus was generous to the peasants

… with a nasty twist or two. He'd give away lottery tickets at the games, where you could win a slave or a house, if you were lucky. If you were unlucky, you got a dead dog or a swarm of bees.

- Once he threw poisonous snakes to the crowds with the lottery tickets, causing deaths by snake bites or trampling.
- It's said he ordered a servant to gather a huge weight of cobwebs. When the slave failed, he had him shut in a cage and eaten alive by dozens of starving rats.

The historian Dio wrote about what happened when the people turned against Elagabalus:

> Elagabalus tried to flee by hiding in a chest in a toilet. But he was discovered and slain, at the age of eighteen. His mother, who clung tightly to him, died with him; their heads were cut off and their bodies, after being stripped naked, were first dragged all over the city, and then stuffed into a sewer. His friends were tortured and had stakes pushed through their bodies.

MURAD IV (1612–40)

Murad IV (ruled in 1623–40) took the throne of Turkey when he was just eleven years old.

The army tried to run the country for him. Mad Murad hated that. He grew up to get revenge and had 500 army leaders strangled.

One of his hobbies was to wander the streets in

disguise to catch anyone making trouble. He had them executed on the spot. Every street corner had a corpse hanging there.

Anyone caught drinking coffee or smoking tobacco was also executed on the spot.

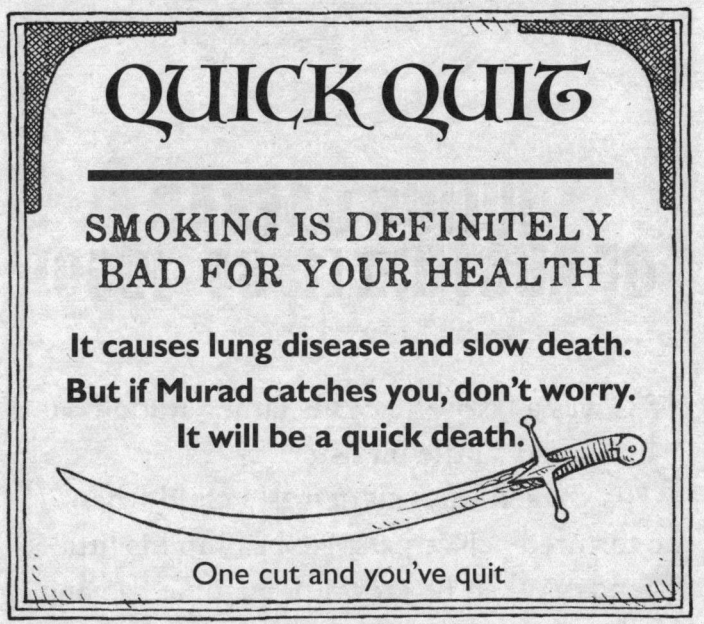

JULIUS CAESAR OF AUSTRIA (1584–1609)

JC was a favourite of his father, Rudolf. He was also a little monster.

His wicked ways started as a child when he tortured palace pets. He beat up his little 'friends'. When he grew up, he joined a gang of young men who brought terror to the peasants. JC's father had him locked in a monastery.

That just made him worse. His father felt sorry for him and set him free. Big mistake.

JC fell in love with the daughter of a poor

barber. When he grew tired of her, he stabbed her with a sword and threw her out of a window. She fell into a soft rubbish heap and lived.

JC asked her to come back to his palace. She refused, so he said…

She went back. Another big mistake. He cut her up into so many pieces she had to be put into her coffin in lots of bits.

In the end JC was locked away and strangled.

THE WORST PALACE IN THE WORLD

HOME, SWEET HOME

THE TOWER OF LONDON

Palaces are lovely places in fairy tales. Not always in real life though.

People think the Tower of London is a place of torture and execution. But for a long time, it was seen as the home of the English kings and queens ... a palace.

AND THERE'S NO PALACE LIKE HOME

When William the Conqueror arrived in 1066, he built the Tower to entertain his lords.

But in 1381 one woman entered the Tower at the head of a peasant army. She was a fearsome woman of Kent, Johanna Ferrour. A chief of the Peasants' Revolt.

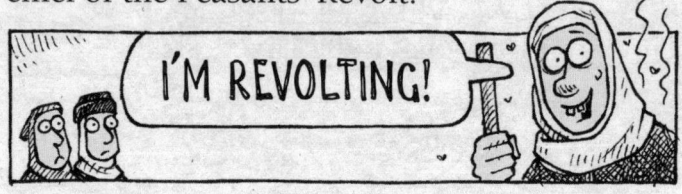

Johanna led an attack on the Tower, where some important victims were trying to hide. They were the Archbishop of Canterbury, Simon Sudbury, and the Lord High Treasurer, Robert Hales.

There were guards at the Tower, but they were scaredy cats. They simply opened the gates and let Johanna and friends in. A report said:

> And at last, the rebels found the Archbishop of Canterbury, called Simon, a brave and wise man. These gluttons took him and struck off his head.

The archbishop had his head forced on to an executioner's block. It took eight blows to hack through his neck. Clearly the peasants hadn't had a lot of practice at the head-chopping lark. That must have hurt.

Simon's mitre (archbishop's hat) was then nailed to his head ... which wouldn't hurt at all. His head was stuck on London Bridge.

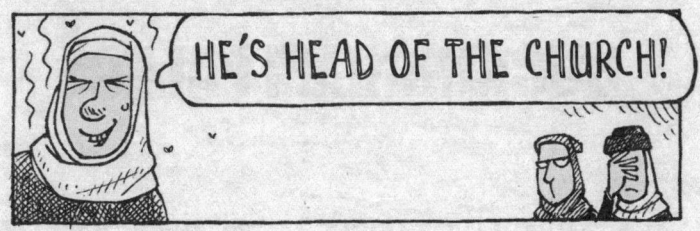

BUCKINGHAM PALACE

William the Conqueror had lived in a house on the spot where Buckingham Palace now stands. But it had been a marsh, so the houses built there were usually damp. William gave the great house away – who can blame him?

King George IV (ruled in 1820–30) was famous for spending money. He rebuilt Buckingham Palace and Windsor Castle, which are still used by the royal family today. He grew so fat the rhyme 'Georgie Porgie pudding and pie' was written about him.

DID YOU KNOW....?

• When the new palace was built it was called 'Buckingham House' because it was built for the Duke of Buckingham in 1703.

• Buckingham House was acquired by King George III in 1761 as a home for Queen Charlotte while he stayed in St James's Palace. It then became known as 'The Queen's House'.

• Fourteen of Charlotte's fifteen children were born there.

• During the 1800s it was patched up and made bigger.

• Queen Victoria (ruled in 1837–1901) was the first British ruler to move into Buckingham Palace ... and it was a real mess. The chimneys smoked all the time, the walls were damp and the stench of rotten food drifted up from the cellar.

• Victoria's staff were lazy, and visitors said the palace was dirty.

SO? AREN'T PALACES FOR THE FILTHY RICH?

In the Second World War Buckingham Palace was bombed. George VI was king at the time and said he was sure that the bomber was his Spanish cousin, the Duke of Galliera.

The queen said…

I'm glad we've been bombed.

She felt they were sharing the suffering of Londoners who were bombed in the Blitz. But some of their people weren't so sure…

VERSAILLES

The French don't have kings these days. But they still look back at some of them and say (in French), 'He was a good guy ... for a king.' And one of their favourites is Louis XIV (ruled in 1643–1715). His nickname was 'The Sun King'.

His vast palace at Versailles cost millions in today's money.

• It had hundreds of fountains and waterspouts in its gardens.

- The palace had golden ceilings and 5,000 servants.

- It only had two toilets. Rich visitors had to take their own potties with them.

- Potties were emptied in a ditch at one corner of the palace – and Louis made sure unpopular guests had their rooms just above that dreadful ditch.

And all the time Louis XIV was there, his French peasants starved.

The later king, Louis XVI, never really wanted to be king. He was shy, clumsy and as silly as some big daft kid. Why not try some of Louis's jolly tricks at school and see how much detention you can get?

1. As servants walked down the Palace corridors, King Louis XVI thought it was fun to trip them up. (Try it with teachers, not your friends.)

2. Louis had servants to dress him. He would take off his clothes so his night servants could hand him his nightshirt. Louis would then pull a silly face and run away naked.

3. Louis would try to make his friends laugh by walking around with his trousers round his ankles.

THE WORST KNIGHT IN THE WORLD

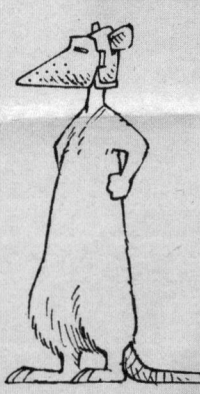

A KNIGHT IN DECLINING ARMOUR

THE BLACK DOUGLAS (1286–1330)

In days of old, knights were bullies and thugs. They rode on horses and chopped down peasants for fun. When they fought other knights, they saw it as a test of their honour – kill or be killed.

In the early 1300s the Scots were fighting to be free of English rule. Black Douglas's grandfather had already died in the wars.

AYE, MURDERED IN AN ENGLISH PRISON

Douglas fought for his leader, Robert the Bruce. Douglas Castle in Dumfries had been seized. He attacked to get it back. He waited till the English defenders were in the castle church. They expected mercy. Douglas expected revenge...

> TAKE THEM TO THE CELLARS AND BEHEAD THEM ALL

In 1314, Douglas came up with a new idea in an attack on Roxburgh Castle. He ordered his men...

> COVER YOURSELVES IN THE SKINS OF COWS AND CRAWL UP TO THE CASTLE AFTER DARK

It worked. The guards thought the attackers were a harmless bunch of cows.

Douglas helped defeat the English at the Battle of Bannockburn then chased them into England. An English soldier complained ...

DOUGLAS WAS SO CLOSE BEHIND WE DIDN'T EVEN DARE STOP FOR A PEE.

He brought terror to the families of the north of England. Then he set off on a pilgrimage.

Douglas was killed fighting in Spain when his army ran off and left him. He wanted to be buried in Scotland but in the summer heat his body would rot and start to smell on the trip home. So, how was he taken back?

a) In a fridge full of mountain ice
b) Boiled till the flesh fell away and his bones taken home
c) In a barrel of vinegar like a pickled egg

Answer: (b) His bones were put in a grave near his family home.

SIMON DE MONTFORT (1175–1218)

- In 1209 Cathar rebels were fighting the Catholic Church in France. Simon de Montfort was sent to sort them out. He pulled out the eyes of the Cathars he caught and sliced off their noses and lips. One man was left with one eye. The one-eyed man was given the job of leading his blind mates to the next Cathar fortress as a warning:

- Simon's excuse for the cruelty was that the Cathars had done the same to two Catholic knights. Other knights had their skin ripped off by Cathars while they were alive, and ordinary soldiers often had hands or feet chopped off.

- Simon de Montfort moved on to Minerve in June 1210 and captured lots of Cathars. Over one hundred of them refused to become Catholics. Sizzling Simon burned all of them on one big bonfire. Some witnesses said the Cathars were so happy to die that the Catholics didn't have to throw them on the bonfire – they threw themselves on.

- The Lady of Lavaur sheltered 400 Cathars and refused to give them up to de Montfort. When she was captured in May 1211 Simon had her thrown down a well and stones piled on top of her. The lady died horribly, but not as horribly as some of her knights. Eighty of them were lined up to be hanged all at once. But the weight was too great and the hanging beam collapsed. They had their throats cut instead.

• The women of a Cathar city used a war catapult to fire a boulder that crushed Simon's skull. Revenge.

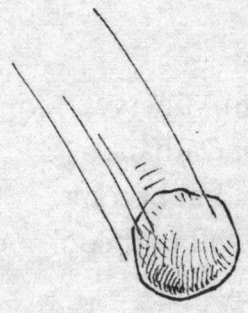

WILLIAM DE TRACY (1135–90)

Knights were supposed to fight the wicked and defend the weak. But William de Tracy murdered an unarmed priest.

Henry I was really upset with the Archbishop of Canterbury, Thomas Becket. Becket said his church had powers over the king of England. Henry cried out in rage…

WHO WILL GET RID OF THIS PROBLEM PRIEST FOR ME?

Will and three friends thought Henry wanted Becket killed. So they set off for Canterbury and attacked Becket in his cathedral. In the struggle one of Becket's clerks, Edward Grim, had his arm almost cut off. A report said:

> A knight planted his foot on Becket's neck and with the point of his sword drew out the blood and brains from the gash of the skull, scattering them on the pavement.

King Henry was sorry. The knights were told to say sorry. William de Tracy was sent to the Holy Land to fight in the Crusades and say sorry in Jerusalem. But the winds were so strong he was blown back. God was not in a mood to forgive William, the Killer of Canterbury.

The church said Will would die a sinner and go to hell ... which is nearly as bad as having your brains scattered over the floor.

THE WORST PANDEMIC IN THE WORLD

AVOID THIS LIKE THE PLAGUE

THE BLACK DEATH (1346–53)

Do you get headaches and feel weak? Do you spit blood and smell terrible? The bad news is you may have bubonic plague – the Black Death. The good news is that four out of every five people only suffer for a week. Then they die and they are too dead to suffer.

An Italian writer called Boccaccio kept a record of the worst terror of all...

> *In men and women there are purple swellings in the groin or armpits. Some grow as large as a common apple, others as large as an egg. They soon begin to spread in all directions and change to black or purple spots on the arm or the thigh or elsewhere. This is a sign of certain death.*

No one could count how many died but it was around half of everyone in the world. Agnolo di Tura wrote...

> Great pits were dug and piled deep with the dead. And people died by the hundreds both day and night. And as soon as those ditches were filled more were dug. And I, Agnolo di Tura, buried my five children with my own hands. So many died we all believed it was the end of the world.

Bodies were loaded on to carts by collectors walking the streets crying...

Fleas were blamed for carrying the plague germs and passing them on when they bit someone. The plague returned in the 1600s. In China it emptied some towns. A writer said...

> At first the bodies were buried in coffins, then in fields and finally they were just left on their beds to rot. There are few signs of human life in the streets. All that can be heard is the buzzing of flies.

The rich ran away to their houses in the country. The poor couldn't do that, so they stayed in their villages and died.

SPANISH FLU (1918–1920)

Five hundred years after the Black Death came the Purple Death. Shivers and fevers and weakness were signs that you had the Spanish flu. The ones who died had dark brown spots on their cheeks which spread till the whole face was purple.

The First World War was cruel, and over 20 million people died in the fighting. But in 1918, as the war came to an end, this new type of flu began to spread. It probably killed over 50 million people. It was far DEADLIER than the war. It was spread from coughs and spits. The *New York Times* newspaper reported...

> # NEW YORK TIMES
>
> ## SCOUT OUT THE SPITTERS
>
> A new law has banned spitting in the street. This is to stop the spread of flu. Boy Scouts in New York City will be looking out for people they see spitting on the street. They will give them cards that read: 'You are breaking the new health law.'

Soldiers had lived through four years of bullets and bombs, mud, machine guns and poison gas shells. Now they started to die from the flu. They crowded on to trains and boats to get home, and that made it spread even faster. A new set of adverts appeared with words we still use a hundred years later...

COUGHS AND SNEEZES SPREAD DISEASES

AND KISSES SPREAD DISISSES

ATHENS PLAGUE (430–426 BC)

It's not always the number of victims that make a plague a disaster. Sometimes it is WHO is killed.

The history writer Thucydides said a plague spread from North Africa and across the Mediterranean. It was so deadly no one could remember anything like it.

> PEOPLE DIED ALONE BECAUSE NO ONE WANTED TO RISK CARING FOR THEM

Athens was at war with the fearsome Sparta. A Spartan army marched into the Athens countryside. People from the country fled to Athens city for safety and, as usual, crowds spread disease.

The Spartans saw the funeral fires.

But it was the death of the Athens leader, Pericles, that hurt the most. Firstly, the people of Athens blamed him for letting so many people into their city. Then he caught the disease and died.

Without Pericles, Athens lost the war against Sparta. The history of the world was changed. By germs.

THE WORST RELIGION IN THE WORLD

AZTEC GODS (1400s)

Many religions have made sacrifices...
- The priests take animals or people and kill them.
- The blood is a gift to their gods.
- In return the gods will be kind to them – often sending good weather to give good crops.

That's the idea. Sometimes the flesh is cooked, and the feast offered to the gods.

Who really ate the cooked meat?

The priests, of course.

But killing people to keep the gods happy – human sacrifice – was nastiest of all. The Aztecs sometimes went to war just to capture victims. Their hearts were torn out at the top of a pyramid.

Then the Spanish arrived from Europe with a different religion, and they were horrified. A Spaniard called Tapia wrote…

> AT THE TOP OF THE PYRAMID WAS A ROOM WITH A STATUE OF THE GREATEST GOD OF ALL THE LAND. IT WAS THREE METRES HIGH. HE WAS MADE FROM SEEDS THAT WERE GROUND UP INTO FLOUR THEN MIXED INTO A PASTE WITH THE BLOOD OF BOYS AND GIRLS.
>
> THE PEOPLE ROSE AT MIDNIGHT TO MAKE THEIR SACRIFICE, WHICH WAS LETTING BLOOD FROM THEIR OWN TONGUES, ARMS AND THIGHS, WETTING STRAWS WITH THE BLOOD AND OFFERING THEM TO A HUGE OAK-WOOD FIRE.

Spaniard Bernal Diaz Del Castillo was most shocked by the 'skull rack' near the main gate to the temple. Hundreds of skulls were set in cement into a sloping wall and seventy tall poles stood on top, each pole with dozens of pegs. Diaz went on...

> Each peg had five skulls on. A total of 136,000 skulls were counted and this did not include the countless skulls that made up the walls.

Still, the Spaniards managed to create their own horrors in that nightmare city. A rebel chief and his sons were brought to the city for execution. It was ordered that they should be burned alive at the stake. The Aztec religion was horrible. But the Spanish Christians weren't much better.

THE CRUSADES (1095–1291)

In 1095 Pope Urban II decided it was time the Christians took over Jerusalem, their Holy Land. Urban tried the usual war-maker's trick of telling his people how cruel the enemy could be.

Raymond of Aguilers wrote a famous diary account of what he had seen:

> Wonderful sights were to be seen. Some of our men (and this was more merciful) cut off the heads of their enemies; others shot them with arrows, so that they fell from the towers; others tortured them longer by casting them into the flames. Piles of heads, hands and feet were to be seen in the streets of the city.

Another knight wrote:

> Our troops boiled enemy adults in cooking pots, and roasted children on spits and ate them grilled.

The Crusaders wrote to the Pope to say 'sorry' for eating people. Pope Urban replied 'I forgive them. God says it is all right to eat a pagan if you are starving.'

The Turks fought back and defeated the

First Crusade in the end. A Second Crusade set out to rescue the first lot. They failed. Then a Third Crusade, with England's King Richard the Lionheart, tried again. Lots of Turks and Christians died horrible deaths but their deaths did not change anything. By 1291, not quite 200 years after the First Crusade, the Christians lost their last city in the Holy Land.

IRELAND (1649)

P eople have killed other people because they worship a different god. But some people worship the same god ... in a different way. So, they fight them. Incredible but true.

In 1649 the Christian Puritans went to war in Ireland because the Christian Catholics were killing Christian Protestants. The Puritan leader in England was Oliver Cromwell. Each side had an excuse...

Cromwell had the power and the ruthless forces to cross to Ireland. He said...

Misery and desolation, blood and ruin, shall fall on the Catholics.

And he made sure it did. When his army attacked Drogheda, they killed all 2,500 defenders. Then they went on to execute priests and anyone else they thought might be dangerous.

Sir Arthur Aston, English Catholic leader of Drogheda's defence, was captured. His wooden leg was ripped off and he was beaten to death with it. Soldiers believed it was full of gold – all they got was splinters.

Priests in Wexford were flogged to death then their bodies were flung into drains. Soldiers often dressed in Catholic priests' clothes to make fun of their victims.

In Wexford 200 women and children were herded into the marketplace to be slaughtered. Cromwell explained, 'This is a judgement from God.' Cromwell's visit is still remembered in Ireland as the Curse of Cromwell.

THE WORST CURE IN THE WORLD

IT'S KILL OR CURE

INCA (1430s)

When you are sick you want a cure. But sometimes the cures are worse than the illness. And others just don't work at all.

HELP! I'M A DOCTOR'S GUINEA PIG

In the 1430s the little Inca tribe in South America started to grow quickly. They would grow to rule the area we now call Peru. They brought with them some curious cures.

CURE THAT KID

DOES YOUR BABY HAVE A FEVER?

COME TO SHOE'S CHEMIST.
WE TRAVEL FAR AND WIDE TO COLLECT HUMAN PEE.

All YOU have to do is wash baby in it.
If that doesn't work, then give it to baby to drink.
Yummy drink from mummy.
Buy one get one pee.
Shoe's Chemist. Sole supplier.

Harmless (probably). But which of these Inca cures would you like to try?

DO YOU SUFFER FROM AWFUL ACHES? LET US CURE YOU. HERE'S HOW...

WE TAKE A GLASS KNIFE AND GOUGE A HOLE BETWEEN YOUR EYES, THIS WILL CURE YOUR HEADACHE IN NO TIME

GEORGIANS (1750s)

Cures didn't get a lot better down the years. The Georgian British suffered some cruel cures.

In the USA tricksters went around selling cures that didn't work. Yet people still bought them. As the American showman PT Barnum said, 'There's a fool born every minute.' The tricksters are known as 'snake oil' salesmen because snake oil doesn't exist. The Georgian snake-oil salesmen came up with these daft cures…

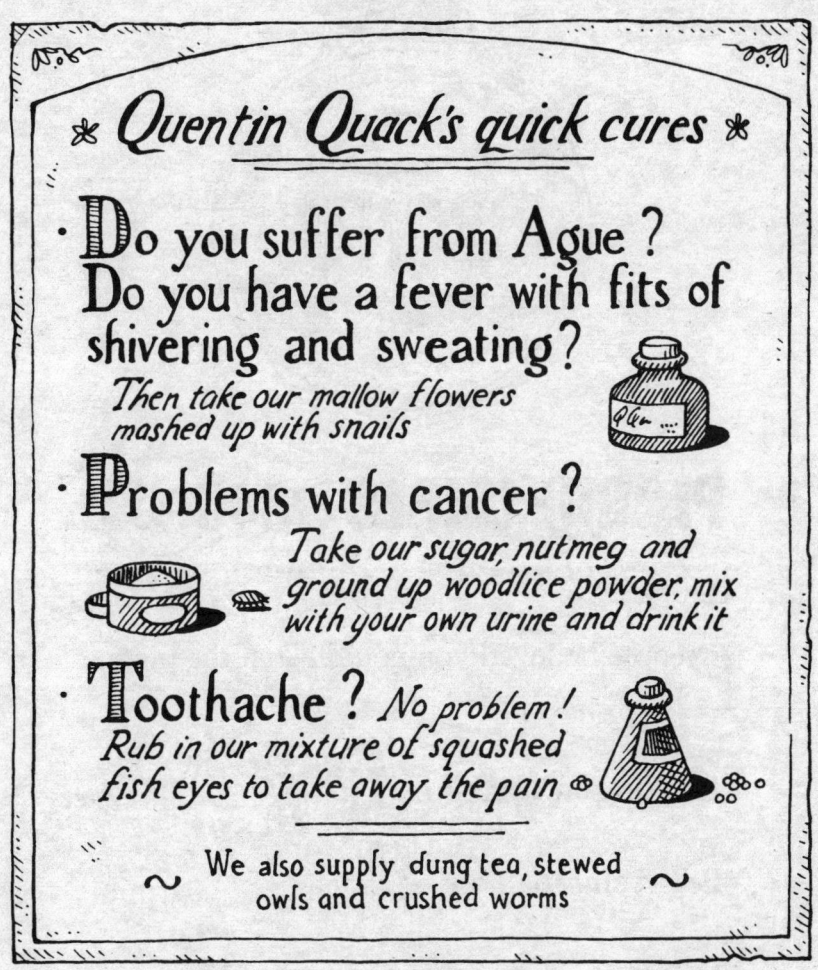

The cures were ALL really tried in Georgian times.

PLAGUE CURES (1346–53)

People believed you could catch the plague by...

- Looking at a victim.

- Breathing bad air.

- Drinking from poisoned wells.

And the cures were almost as dreadful as the disease. Doctors already had some wacky cures for illnesses. They said...

- Throw sweet-smelling herbs on a fire to clean the air.

- Sit in a sewer so the bad air of the plague is driven off by the worse air of the drains.

- Drink a medicine of ten-year-old treacle.

- Swallow powders of crushed emeralds (for the rich).

- Eat arsenic powder (highly poisonous).

- Try letting blood out of the patient (when the patient's horoscope was right).

- Kill all the cats and dogs in the town.

Best of all ...
- Shave a live chicken's bottom and strap it to the plague sore. The disease flows from the sore into the chicken. (And if it doesn't work you can still enjoy a chicken supper.)

THE WORST ENSLAVER IN THE WORLD

CHRISTOPHER COLUMBUS (1451–1506)

Christopher Columbus was an Italian explorer. He is famous for discovering America (which wasn't even lost at the time). He was probably the worst thing ever to happen to the Indigenous Americans.

Chris and his Spanish masters wanted gold, land, gold, people to enslave … and gold. That's what they got. The land and the gold belonged to the Indigenous Americans, of course, but that didn't matter to the savage Spanish. The invasion cost Chris very little – it cost the Indigenous Americans everything.

Chris was followed by invaders – conquistadors. One of them wrote…

> *At daybreak great multitudes of men came to the shore. I listened very carefully to them and tried to find out if they had any gold. I gathered from their signs that if I sailed south I would find a king with great cups full of gold. I could conquer all of these people with just fifty men and rule them as I please.*

When Chris set off for home he kidnapped around twenty Indigenous Americans. The terrible conditions on the ships meant only around seven arrived in Spain alive. They were enough to show the Spanish that these strong people would make great workers.

Chris headed back to America a second time – and this time he had over 1,200 soldiers armed with guns, swords, cannons and attack dogs.

In 1495 the Spanish rounded up over 1,600 Arawaks on Haiti to either be sent back to Spain or taken to work for them on the islands. Half the islanders died on the journey, but Chris shrugged and said...

Although they die now, they will not always die. We can send all the slaves from here that you can sell.

But he was wrong. Forced work and dreadful diseases killed ALL the Arawaks off.

When the Arawaks tried to fight back in 1495, Chris sent heavily armed soldiers to mow them down. His son Ferdinand wrote about his dreadful dad and said...

The most terrible weapons were the twenty attack dogs who immediately tore the Indigenous Americans apart. These animals ripped open the limbs and bellies and chased fleeing Indigenous Americans into the bush.

The Indigenous Americans who were captured alive were simply killed. There were around three million Arawaks on Haiti when Chris arrived in 1492. Sixty years later there were almost none.

ELIZABETH I (1533–1603)

The Pope said his followers in Spain and Portugal could take people from Africa to work for Spanish and Portuguese enslavers…

The Spanish and Portuguese rushed across the Atlantic to find fortunes in gold and silver. They needed more people than ever to work in the mines and paid good prices to buy them.

The English queen, Elizabeth I, wanted part of that rich trade for herself. Sir Francis Drake – her top captain – was the man for the job. In 1567, Drake made one of the first English slaving voyages as part of a fleet led by his cousin John Hawkins, shipping African people across to America. The Spanish were furious.

In 1585 the queen gave Drake £20,000 – half of the cost of new ships and supplies – to send him back to Africa and South America.

The Spanish were ready for him this time and he was beaten time and again. He returned with just £30,000 in treasure – £15,000 for Queen Liz. So, she lost £5,000. Drake lost 750 men, including some of his best captains.

But the misery of the British slave trade had started. Thanks Liz.

THE ROMANS (700s BC)

The Roman Empire needed people to work for them like no empire before. Enslaved people did dozens of different jobs…

- Gladiators (deadly)
- Miners (even deadlier)
- Hairdressers (not quite so dangerous)
- Teachers (deadliest of all)

> **HORRIBLE HISTORIES Warning:**
> Roman fathers could sell their children as slaves (so don't let your parents read this, they may get ideas).

The Romans were always worried that their slaves would run away. They had men whose jobs were to catch them. They made laws that said…

> **A runaway slave may be whipped, burned with iron or killed.**

And many people were forced to wear iron collars with words stamped onto them. One said:

> I HAVE RUN AWAY. CATCH ME. IF YOU TAKE ME BACK TO MY MASTER ZONINUS, YOU'LL BE REWARDED.

THE WORST WOMEN IN THE WORLD

FATAL FEMMES FATALES

ELIZABETH BATHORY
(1560–1614)

If Elizabeth had a police record it may have looked like this…

NAME: Elizabeth Bathory, 'The Blood Countess of Transylvania' (that's part of Romania, if you are looking for somewhere cheerful to spend your next holiday).

CRUEL CRIMES: Bloody Bess was born in 1560 into one of the richest families in Transylvania. She should have had a happy life — but she killed over 600 women and girls in the early 1600s. Why? So she could have a bath in their blood. She thought it made her look young. Bloodthirsty Bess had four horrible henchmen to help her. They drained the blood from the victims and filled the baths. But one of her victims escaped and told the law officers about what was happening at Cachtice Castle. On 30 December 1610 they raided that house of horror and were horrified by the terrible sights in the castle — in the dungeon they discovered several living girls, some of whose bodies had been half drained of blood. Dead girls had been thrown to the wolves.

In the winter she executed victims by having their clothes taken away, then having them led out into the snow and soaked with water until they froze.

Bad Bess never went on trial and was never found guilty. Her four servants were executed – beheaded and burned after having their fingers torn off – but Bess was simply put out of harm's way.

Stonemasons were brought to Cachtice Castle to brick up the windows and doors of the bedroom with the countess inside. They left a small hole through which food could be passed. She stayed there for the rest of her life and died in the castle in 1614. Servants said she tortured and killed about fifty girls – Elizabeth kept a diary, and that said it was 600.

Johannes Ujvary, Elizabeth's butler, said…

> ABOUT THIRTY-SEVEN GIRLS HAVE BEEN KILLED. SIX OF THEM WERE TAKEN TO THE CASTLE BY ME. THE VICTIMS WERE TIED UP AND CUT WITH SCISSORS. SOMETIMES TWO FRIENDS OF THE COUNTESS TORTURED THESE GIRLS. SOMETIMES THE COUNTESS HERSELF DID IT

> MY TURN

AMINA, NIGERIAN QUEEN OF ZAZZAU (1533–1610)

Amina was a warrior queen, and the stories about her make her sound ruthless and cruel. Amina was mad about training to be a warrior and became as good as any soldier in Nigeria. She started leading her brother's armies at the age of sixteen.

She became queen at the age of forty-three when her brother died.

For the next thirty-four years, she won wars and set off to conquer her neighbours. Her first message as queen was...

My people. Sharpen your weapons.

As a queen there were lots of men wanting to marry her. One brought a rich gift...

Every time her army captured a town, she found herself a new boyfriend from that town. Lucky man? Not really. She wasn't going to share her power with any man.

After one night she had the man beheaded the next morning.

LUCREZIA BORGIA
(1480–1519)

Lucrezia was an Italian duchess. Her father was Pope Alexander VI and her brother was called Cesare. It's said she helped them with their many crimes. It's SAID that she wore a ring that was filled with poison.

GOT A PROBLEM PERSON IN YOUR LIFE?

GIVE THEM A RING.

My hollow ring holds a tasty poison
Slip it into their wine and watch them die

Alexander VI and Cesare were greedy and ruthless. Italy's great crime family. Was Lucrezia part of their plotting? Or did they just use her? Some historians think this poison ring story may not be true.

• In 1493 (at the age of thirteen) she was married off to Giovanni Sforza. That meant Alex and Cesare were now part of the Sforza family, the dukes of Milan. Lucrezia divorced Giovanni four years later when Alexander decided he could find her an even more powerful husband.

• Her second husband was Alfonso of Aragon. In 1500 Alfonso was wounded by four attackers. He went to bed to recover. No chance. He was strangled in bed by one of Cesare's servants.

• Lucrezia took a boyfriend, Pedro Calderon. That didn't suit Cesare. Pedro became dead-ro and his corpse was found floating in the river Tiber at Rome.

• Third time lucky? In 1501 Alfonso d'Este became her third husband. She left Rome to live with him and left her baby son behind. She never saw the child again.

• She gave birth to eight children with Alfonso but died soon after having their ninth child. Lucrezia had packed a lot into her thirty-nine years.

Was she a murderer? Or was she just part of the power game Alexander VI and Cesare were playing? If so, was Lucrezia just the football?

THE WORST JOB IN THE WORLD

SOMEONE'S GOT TO DO IT

GROOM OF THE STOOL (1509–47)

King Henry VIII liked to show off. He wore the finest clothes and jewellery, had the best palaces and dozens of servants to do as he told them.

He also liked to give important visitors a great feast. Many of his people were starving, but Henry's tables were loaded.

MORE FOR ME

One feast had a menu like this...

FIRST COURSE:

Grilled Beaver Tails, Whale Meat, Wild Boar Meat, Roast Tongue, Leg of Pork, Roast Beef, Roast Deer, Meat Pie and Vegetables with Bread and Wine

SECOND COURSE:

Whole Roasted Peacock, Roast Lamb, Swan, Rabbit, Bread, Sugared Fruit, Gingerbread, Sugared Almonds, Spiced Fruitcake

You know that putting a lot of food in your mouth means it has to come out at the other end. You need to poo.

Henry's room had a 'stool' – a toilet bowl inside a wooden box. The 'Groom of the Stool' had to make sure it was always kept fresh and empty. He also had to help the king to wipe his bottom. A hundred years before Henry took the throne there was a rhyme written to tell Grooms of the Stool what their job was…

> See that the toilet is fair, sweet and clean;
> See that the stool has a cover so green;
> Make sure the cover lets no board be seen;
> And there's a soft cushion where royal end has been.
> Let there be linen to wipe of his bowel.
> Fresh water and basin, and carry a towel.

It sounds a smelly job. But in fact it was a top job in the Tudor palaces.

MUDLARK (1800s)

....

Some London children made their living by collecting anything valuable that wound up in the River Thames. They usually waited for low tide before they waded through the slimiest mud to search for treasures dropped in the river. And that 'mud' was full of toilet sewage.

Mudlarks were mostly young boys, though girls and old women could be seen there too plodding knee-deep in the filth. It was tiring work for little reward – a mudlark could hope to find coal, scrap metal and firewood. To find coins or anything valuable was rare.

The two main dangers were:

1) **'Toshers'** – men who hunted in the filth inside the sewers and who weren't gentle in snatching your finds.

2) **Disease** – from any small wound picked up while wading in the poisonous mud. A cut could equal a death sentence.

MATCH MAKING (1880s)

Making matches meant dipping the wooden sticks into phosphorus ... the explosive bit on the end. But contact with poisonous white phosphorus was the cause of 'phossy jaw'.

This disease ate at the makers' jawbones, leaving them with empty cheeks that oozed foul-smelling liquid. It could also cause brain damage and eventually death.

The disease could rip off a girl's jaw – they were usually girls – and lead to a massive infection and a slow, painful death.

THIS JOB MAKES ME SICK!

A group of girls working in a London factory held a strike in 1888 and were successful in replacing white phosphorus with the safer 'red' phosphorus.

RED NOT DEAD

In 1891 the Salvation Army opened up its own match factory using red phosphorus and paying better wages. But there were still young homeworkers, using white phosphorus to their cost. Several younger children in their families died from eating these matches.

THE WORST JOURNEY IN THE WORLD

IN THE WORLD

A TRIP DOWN
MISERY LANE

MAGELLAN (1480–1521)

Ferdinand Magellan is famous. He was the first person to sail around the world. Except he didn't. He may have set off to sail around the world, but he died before he got back.

Magellan was from Portugal and wanted to find a way to sail west to get to the east. It would help with the rich spice trade. Spain paid him to try it. A writer called Pigafetta was sent along to report on the trip. His notes must have been interesting.

September 1519
Five ships and enough supplies for two years at sea. A great leader, Ferdinand Magellan. Nothing can go wrong.

December 1519
Arrived on coast of South America. There had been no rain here for two months until we reached the port and it poured. The natives thought we brought a miracle. We told them it was our God and converted them into Christians.

April 1520
Oh dear. The Spanish crews are revolting. Captain Mendoza has been killed in a mutiny. The great Magellan blames two other captains. He sentenced Captain Quesada to be beheaded; Captain Cartagena has been marooned. The bodies of the mutineers were cut into quarters and put on show. No one beats Magellan.

October 1520

We sent the ship Santiago to find a way around the south of America. It was wrecked by winter storms. We sent Captain Mesquita to find a way. His crew rebelled and sailed the ship back to Spain. We have just three ships left but the great Magellan will get us through.

November 1520

Wonderful news. We have found our way into the western ocean we call Pacific. Crews are falling ill with scurvy. Nearly fifty crew dead or dying of starvation. We ate old biscuits reduced to powder, full of maggots and stinking from rat droppings. Not so wonderful. Magellan carries on.

April 1521

Disaster. Magellan attacked a tribe on Mactan Island with fifty men. Our sailors carried guns and wore armour, but 1,500 islanders swarmed over them. They killed our leader with spears and swords. They refused to hand over his body. So ended the life of Magellan, our mirror, our light, our comfort and our true guide.

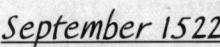

September 1522

The last ship, Victoria, arrived back in Spain three years after she set off. She carried eighteen men — 270 had set off. But we did what Magellan said was possible, and sailed around the world. No one had ever done it before.

JAMES COOK (1728–79)

An explorer sails around the world. He lands on an island and is killed by the inhabitants. Have you heard that story before? The captain's name wasn't Magellan, it was Cook. This was James Cook, and it was over 250 years after Magellan had died. Some people just don't learn from *Horrible Histories*.

Cook was a British naval captain who led three famous voyages between 1768 and 1779 in the Pacific ocean. Cook's crew were some of the first people from Europe to set eyes on Australia.

On his third trip Cook's ship snapped a mast. He came ashore at Hawaii to fix it and that's when things went wrong. Badly wrong.

- Cook sent his men to fetch wood and they stole it from a Hawaiian graveyard so…
- The Hawaiians pinched one of *Endeavour*'s rowing boats so…
- Cook set out to capture both the boat AND the Hawaiian chief so…
- Cook took the chief from his home and led him away to the waiting boat so…
- The Hawaiians clubbed Cook over the head and stabbed him at the edge of the sea.

The Hawaiians treated Cook's body with respect. They baked it so the flesh would come off and leave his skeleton. Unlike Magellan's killers, they gave Cook's crew a few bones to take back home.

fig.1
Cook's cooked clavicle

CAPTAIN SCOTT
(1868–1912)

Captain Cook sailed so far south he almost reached the Antarctic. He turned back. It was too cold. (No surprise if you're a penguin.)

In 1912 Captain Robert Scott led a team of Britons all the way to the South Pole. It was a race against a Norwegian expedition led by Roald Amundsen.

Did Scott's group make it to the South Pole? Yes. Did they win the race? No. Amundsen's men got there first.

Scott and his men died of the cold and exhaustion on the way back. Some people have said it was because Scott used ponies to pull his sledges – the ponies died, and the Brits had to pull their own supplies. Amundsen used trained dogs.

One of Scott's men, Lawrence Oates, decided to walk out into the frozen ice and die. He thought his frostbite made him so slow the others would be held back. His famous last words were…

I AM JUST GOING OUTSIDE, I MAY BE SOME TIME

The body of Oates has never been found. Scott's diary said, 'We knew it was the act of a brave man and an English gentleman.'

Scott and the last two explorers froze in their tent on 29 March 1912. They were found eight months later and buried under the tent.

Two weeks after Scott died, RMS *Titanic* sank. Not a good month for Britain.

THE WORST RULERS IN THE WORLD

THRONE ALONE

IVAN THE TERRIBLE (TSAR FROM 1547–84)

Ivan wasn't just 'bad'. He was terrible. He was the ruler of Russia.

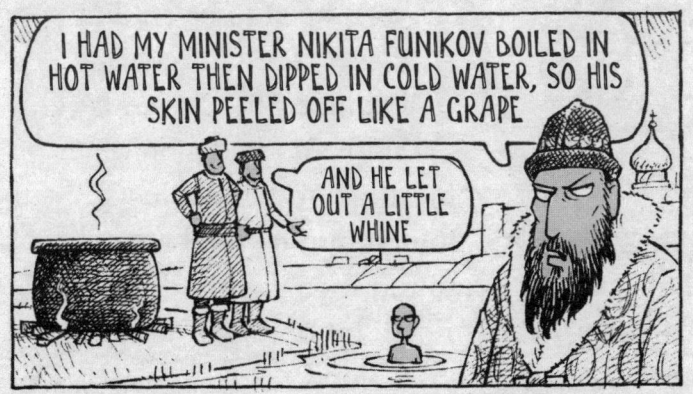

See what I mean? Funikov but not funi.

Ivan the Terrible wanted to control the great lords of Russia – the 'boyars' – in the 1560s. What did he do to them?

a) Gave the boyars a good talking to
b) Locked the boyars in prison until they agreed to do as they are told
c) Had his special police kill the boyars by drowning or strangling or flogging them to death or roasting them on a spit or frying them in large frying pans

Answer: Oh, come on. This is a *Horrible Histories* book. If you said (a) or (b) maybe you need to be reading *Noddy Has a Lovely Day*. Of course, the answer is (c). Old Ivan liked a bit of hunting. You could have joined him if you'd been around then … and didn't mind a bit of blood. Peasant girls' blood…

> Tonight at the palace
>
> # THE HORRIBLE HEN PARTY
>
> **BRING YOUR BOWS AND ARROWS.**
>
> Peasant girls will be stripped and set loose to chase live hens ...
>
> ... while you shoot at them with bows and arrows. If she catches a hen, she goes free ...
>
> ... unless you shoot her first.

Ivan got through more wives than Henry VIII. Some say his seventh wife was Maria Dolgorukaya. It seems awful Maria had had another boyfriend Ivan didn't know about. When the furious feller found out, he had his new bride drowned.

Wife number five, Anna Wassilchikura, found herself a new boyfriend – and Ivan found out. The lucky lass was packed off to a nunnery. But not before the bat-brained boyfriend was stuck on a spike and left to die slowly – outside Anna's palace window.

Ivan's enemy, Prince Boris Telupa, was spiked on a wooden pole – he took fifteen hours to die and talked through it to his mother, who had been forced to watch.

Ivan carried a wooden pole with a metal spike on to lash out at people who annoyed him. One day he lashed out at his own son and killed him. Deadly sort of dad to have. Terrible, in fact.

HENRY VIII
(RULED IN 1509–47)

Henry is famous for having six wives, divorcing two and beheading two.
*Divorced, beheaded, died,
divorced, beheaded, survived.*
Or another way to remember is with a jolly song…

> Cathy of Aragon was his first wife,
> He gave the poor woman a load of strife.
> Cath and the fat man had no boy kids,
> so that put their marriage on the skids.

Henry, he married Anne Boleyn,
but Anne was a lively lass and she did sin.
She went to her death with a swish
of a sword, the women in his life were
never bored.
Henry then married Jane Seymour,
she was the one he really adored.
She gave him a son and she dropped down
dead; he didn't have a lot of luck it must
be said.
Anne of Cleves his fourth, of course,
but when he saw her face he said,
'She's a horse.'
So Henry he gave Anne a sad divorce,
which wasn't little Annie's fault, of course.
Catherine Howard was number five,
the cold axe she just could not survive.
Cath Parr was six – her lucky number,
because she saw fat Henry six feet under.

SHAKA, ZULU CHIEF (RULED IN 1816–28)

Great warrior, nasty man. When Shaka's mother became pregnant, she said, 'It's not a baby, it's *ishaka*.' And *ishaka* means a pain in the stomach. When the baby was born, he was known as Shaka, after his mother's moan.

But Shaka caused more than a gut-ache to many people. He killed his father and took over the leadership of the Zulu nation. Then he was terrified of growing old. He believed that having children aged a man. He had 1,200 wives but any babies that were born were murdered at birth along with their mothers.

When Shaka's mum died, he was so upset he ordered hundreds to be slaughtered. Somehow this maniac made the Zulu nation huge and powerful. But his violence grew out of control and most of his people were happy when he was speared to death by his half-brother. By then a million Zulu had died in his 'terror'.

THE WORST TORTURERS IN THE WORLD

THIS IS GOING TO HURT...

WILLIAM WAAD
(1546–1623)

Guy Fawkes was a terrorist to Protestants and a freedom fighter to Catholics. The question is, 'Why try to blow King James sky high, Guy?'

Because (Guy would tell you) King James was just as bad as the old queen, Elizabeth, when it came to killing Catholics.

THEY DIDN'T SIMPLY EXECUTE THEM. THEY TORTURED CAPTURED CATHOLICS TO GIVE AWAY SECRETS AND BETRAY FRIENDS

- Of course, Queen Elizabeth and King James DIDN'T torture Catholic victims. Not themselves. They got a top man to do it. The Tower of London governor, William Waad.

- William Waad was made governor of the Tower of London eleven weeks before Guy Fawkes was imprisoned there. Waad was an expert at torturing prisoners.

- A Catholic priest called Gerard had been brought to Waad for torturing. Gerard lived to tell his own story of his torture…

> They led me to a great pillar of wood that was one of the supports of this vast crypt.
>
> At the top were staples, and here they placed my wrists in manacles of iron. They ordered me to mount two or three steps.
>
> My arms being fixed above my head, they withdrew those steps one by one so that I hung by my hands and arms.
>
> Thus hanging by the wrists they asked me if I was willing to confess. I replied, 'I cannot, I will not.'

> *But so terrible was the pain that I was hardly able to speak. The worst pain was in my chest and belly, my arms and hands.*
>
> *It seemed to me that all the blood in my body had rushed up to my arms and hands.*

Gerard fainted after an hour, was woken with cold water and hung up again till he fainted again. This happened about seven or eight times that afternoon.

Brave Gerard suffered three days of this treatment before he managed to escape with the help of a rope from the Tower. His hands were mangled from the tortures he had suffered yet he managed to climb down.

That was what Guy Fawkes faced. King James wanted to give the plotter a chance to confess. He told Waad…

> THE GENTLER TORTURES ARE TO BE USED FIRST ON HIM AND THEN GRADUALLY GO TO THE HARDEST

Fawkes held out bravely for several days. He named the other plotters, but he had given them time to escape from London.

THOMAS OF TORQUEMADA (1420–98)

William Waad would tell you the Catholics were ace at torturing too. Their most famous torturer was a Spanish monk called Thomas of Torquemada.

The Catholic Church in Spain said that anyone who wasn't a Catholic was a 'heretic'. They could get out of the country with just the clothes they were wearing. The man in charge of punishing these heretics was Torquemada.

Two thousand people died in his reign of terror. They were tortured then sent to be burned alive.

Two years after he died Torquemada's grave was robbed and his bones burned to ash.

MATTHEW HOPKINS (1620–47)

In the 1600s, a fear of witches swept the world. And where there is fear there is someone ready to make money. In the east of England it was a young man called Matthew Hopkins.

In three years (1644 to 1647) his work led to more people being hanged as witches than in the hundred years before. He saw 400 executed – mostly women.

The more 'witches' he found the more money he made. It was against the law to torture anyone in England in that age. Hopkins found ways to do it by…

• Keeping the victim awake for days till they said, 'Yes, I'm a witch.'

• 'Pricking' a mark on the witch's body to see if they bled – if it didn't bleed it was the 'Devil's Mark' and they were sent for trial.

Hopkins said, 'The pricking was a trick on my part. The pin I used had a hollow handle and the needle didn't go into the flesh – it just appeared to. The judges in Bury St Edmunds believed our lies and sent the witches to hang. Eighteen hanged in Bury on one day alone.'

• Swimming … the victim was thrown into the water with hands tied. If they floated they were guilty – the Devil was helping. They were hanged. If they sank, they were innocent … but then they often drowned.

THE WORST CASTLES IN THE WORLD

TOWER POWER

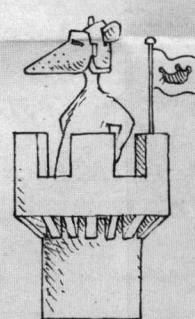

HYLTON CASTLE (1606)

Dungeons and drafts, feasts and fears, moats and minstrels, sieges and spooks. Castles have them all. But some are nastier than others.

At Hylton Castle, near Sunderland in northeast England, there was a murder that echoes down the ages to today. The victim's ghost cries out that he's cold or 'ca'ad' in the local accent.

> ROBIN SKELTON WAS A STABLE LAD AT LORD HYLTON'S CASTLE. BUT HE FELL ASLEEP WHEN HE WAS SUPPOSED TO BE GETTING A HORSE GROOMED. HEAR HIS SAD SONG...

I WORKED IN THE STABLE, BUT I FELL ASLEEP,
HIS LORDSHIP FOUND ME DOZING IN A BIG STRAW HEAP.
HE WHIPPED ME AND HE KICKED ME TILL HE MADE ME WEEP,
THEN HE CHUCKED ME INTO THE POND SO DEEP.

LORD HYLTON THREW ROBIN'S BODY INTO THE CASTLE POND AND THE BOY'S GHOST CAME BACK TO HAUNT THE PLACE.

IF YOU GO TO HYLTON THEN YOU'LL BE THRILLED,
GO ALONG THERE WHEN THE NIGHT AIR'S STILLED.
OLD HYLTON HE DID BEAT ME TILL I WAS KILLED.
LISTEN HARD AND HEAR ME MOAN, 'I'M CHILLED.'

THE BODY WAS FOUND AND HYLTON WAS TRIED FOR ROBIN'S MURDER. BUT HE WAS A LORD. SO THE JUDGE, HIS FRIEND, SAID, 'NOT GUILTY.' THAT'S WHY ROBIN WARNS...

I'M CA'AD, I'M CA'AD, I'M SO CA'AD,
I'M SLIMY AND CLAMMY AS A LUMP OF LARD.
IF YOU WORK FOR HYLTON BE ON YOUR GUARD,
HE HITS YOU WITH A WHIP AND HE HITS YOU HARD.

Britain has more than 4,000 castles (or ruins of castles) and hundreds of horrible haunting stories. There are…

- Nuns thrown down a well
- Queens who have been beheaded
- Giant black dogs…
- … and endless 'grey lady' ghosts

LEAP CASTLE, IRELAND (1250)

Leap Castle has so many ghosts they must be tripping over one another. It has…

• **The Bloody Chapel:** a priest called Thaddeus O'Carroll was holding a service in his family chapel. His brother Teige burst in and plunged a sword through him.

• **The Murder Hole:** it was once filled with hundreds of human skeletons. Many of the skeletons were set on wooden spikes.

- **The Red Lady**: she was held hostage by the O'Carroll family when she had a baby. The O'Carrolls killed it, and the Red Lady wanders the castle nightly, with a knife, looking for the killers.

- **The Elemental**: a spirit that can appear as a man with rotting flesh. And he brings along the smell with him.

- **The Darby Ghost**: the owner hid his money from thieves, then went mad and forgot where he put it. He wanders the castle seeking it.

- **The Priest's House**: go to bed there and something heavy lies beside you and snores. A monk can be seen at the window.

- **The Wall Fall**: Emily died aged eleven after falling from the castle's wall. She is seen again falling off the castle roof and disappears before she hits the ground.

Now you know you will look before you Leap.

MOOSHAM CASTLE, AUSTRIA (1675)

Some say Moosham Castle is the 'most haunted castle in the world'.

From 1675 to 1690 Austria's most grisly witch trials were held at Moosham Castle. One hundred and thirty men and twenty-six women were accused and found guilty of witchcraft. Most of them were beggars and the homeless. There was no one to care about them, no family to stand up for them.

Around forty children aged ten to fourteen died horribly here. Margarethe was the oldest and was executed as a witch at the age of eighty.

The victims could be marked with a hot iron and paraded in front of the local people to show them what happened to witches.

A hundred years later, cattle and deer were found slaughtered near the castle. The peasants said the answer was clear…

YOU know werewolves are nonsense, but some of the castle workers were executed for the crime of being a werewolf.

THE WORST ROBBER IN THE WORLD

THICK AS THIEVES

TWM SIÔN CATI (1530–1609)

The English love Robin Hood, the Scots admire Rob Roy. They are both bandits who lived outside the law. In Wales the great hero outlaw is a man from Tregaron called Twm Siôn Cati.

He is better known in English as Tom Jones.

Twm (unlike Robin Hood) was a real man who lived near Tregaron. Most of the stories told about him have been invented. Stories like this one…

DID YOU KNOW...?

There is a cave between Tregaron and Llandovery which is known as Twm Siôn Cati's cave. Some people say it was the robber's. His sort of fave cave.

NED KELLY (1854-80)

Australian Ned Kelly seemed to end up being an outlaw by accident...

• Constable Fitzpatrick went to the Kelly home to arrest Ned's brother Dan for horse stealing. He was shot in the wrist by Ned, defending his brother. This made Ned Kelly an outlaw.

• Ned and his gang ambushed police at Stringybark Creek. Three policemen were shot and the Kelly gang were to be hanged if they were caught.

- There was a hotel siege at Glenrowan, where in 1880 three members of the Kelly gang were shot dead. Ned wore a suit of body armour made from a steel plough.

- He wore a helmet but forgot to wear armour on his legs. That's where the police shot him, and he was captured. His excuse for killing police?

> I HAD TO SHOOT THEM, OR LIE DOWN AND LET THEM SHOOT ME, SCATTERING PIECES OF ME AND MY BROTHER ALL OVER THE BUSH

- The judge told Kelly he would go to hell. Kelly said, 'I'll see you there, then.'

- The robber's last words before they hanged him were, 'Ah well, I suppose it had to come to this.' Then he died.

Now that's cool. Kelly made a mistake forgetting leg armour ... but cool.

CARL GUGASIAN (1947–)

Carl didn't make mistakes. He became known as the 'Friday Night Bank Robber' because he had a plan, a system that let him escape the law … until he was caught by bad luck.

```
Carl Gugasian:
Want to know how to get
away with it? Here's my
system...
1. Use street maps to pick
small town banks which
```

are next to wooded areas and near motorway junctions.
2. Watch the bank carefully to see how the bank staff come and go.
3. Plan the robbery for autumn or winter when it gets dark early.
4. Rob the banks on Friday nights when there are few customers but lots of cash.
5. Wear a mask, jump over the bank counter with a gun and stuff cash in a bag. Make a hiding place in the woods for the cash, masks and maps.
6. Ride off through the woods on a motorbike and load it into a van at the far side. Go back for the cash later.

He robbed more than fifty banks in America over thirty years for a total of more than $2 million. But two kids were playing in the woods and found his hiding place. That led the police to him, and he went to prison for seventeen years.

THE WORST WARS IN THE WORLD

WHIZZZZZ!

THE THIRTY YEARS' WAR (1618–48)

Where did the Roman Empire go? It split into East and West. The western part disappeared, but later kings in the area of what we now call Holland, Germany and Austria revived a version of it. In that area there were dozens of little states with their own rulers. It became known as the Holy Roman Empire.

The states chose their emperor – usually from the Catholic Habsburg family – and the Pope crowned him. But emperors allowed

Protestants to worship freely ... until 1618.

Catholic lords began closing Protestant churches. Count von Thurn (a Protestant) spoke at a meeting in the Royal Castle of Prague with the Catholic lords...

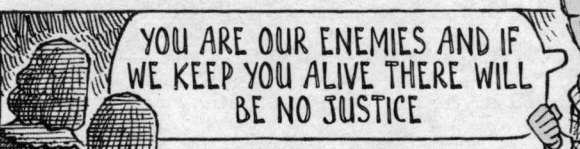

YOU ARE OUR ENEMIES AND IF WE KEEP YOU ALIVE THERE WILL BE NO JUSTICE

The quickest way to get rid of the Catholic lords was to throw them from the windows to the ground, twenty metres below. Two Catholic lords and their secretary made the flight down without a lift or wings.

OUR REVOLT IS OFF TO A FLYING START

The Catholic lords were injured, yet they didn't die. Two lived to run away. How? The victims landed on a dungheap of human waste.

That sparked the Thirty Years' War, Protestant rebels against Catholic lords. The Thirty Years' War has been called the worst war in European history. The nations lost over a quarter of their people to fighting, but also to famine and disease. The war cost nearly as many lives as the Black Death.

Cities became empty. The Swedish army alone destroyed 1,500 German towns, 18,000 villages and 2,000 castles. Soldiers ate the crops, killed the cattle for food and tore down houses to make their fires. The peasants starved or ate corpses from the graveyards. A report said...

The living crawled out from under the dead, crying children wandered the streets calling for their parents. They ate rats to stay alive.

Around 350,000 soldiers died in the battles of the Thirty Years' War. But TWENTY times as many ordinary people died.

DID YOU KNOW ...?

Holy Roman Emperors could be unholy. In Prague in 1398, the Holy Roman Emperor was Wenceslas. His cook failed to make him a good meal, so Wicked Wenceslas had the cook roasted over his own fire.

THE FIRST WORLD WAR (1914–18)

After thousands of years of humans fighting humans, this war would see humans fighting machines … the machine gun, the aeroplane and the tank.

It was also a war that gave us songs and poems. Men were told to go and risk their lives in jolly songs.

```
You'll never find we fail you,
    when you are in distress,
So, answer when we hail you,
```

and let your word be 'Yes',
And so your name, in years to come
Each mother's son shall bless.

Oh we don't want to lose you but we
think you ought to go
For your King and Country both
need you so;

We shall want you and miss you
but with all our might and main
We shall cheer you, thank you, kiss
you, when you come back again.

That's nice. When you come home we shall cheer and thank and kiss you. But what happened if they DIDN'T come home? They were buried and their grave became 'home'. A famous poet, Rupert Brooke, wrote that if he died…

TIMUR'S WARS (1370–1405)

Timur started life as a bandit, and went on to be one of the deadliest warlords EVER. He walked with a limp so he was sometimes called Timur the Lame (or Tamburlaine). Was he a fibber?

Timur enjoyed conquering new lands and he often flattened great cities, but he did also enjoy building. His favourite building was a tower made from the skulls of his victims.

A writer said that in Isfahan, Persia, Timur's warriors massacred the people. Timur built twenty-eight towers with 1,500 skulls in each. In Delhi 50,000 people were killed and their skulls stacked in each corner of the city.

His war killed nearly 20 million people. But why would someone be so keen to use human heads?

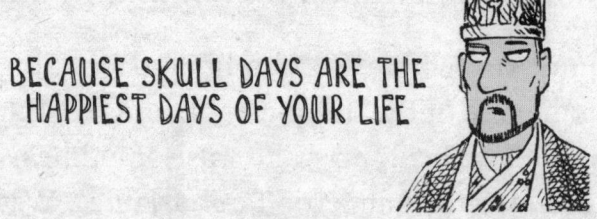

BECAUSE SKULL DAYS ARE THE HAPPIEST DAYS OF YOUR LIFE

HE SHOULD HAVE STUCK TO STEALING SHEEP

THE WORST PIRATE IN THE WORLD

NOT SUCH A JOLLY ROGER

WILLIAM FLY
(DIED c. 1726)

Fly was a small man – not as small as a fly but not much bigger than a boy. He may have been a prize-fighter – boxing without gloves – before he turned to sailing, but sailing seemed to be a better way to get rich quick.

Fly signed on to sail with Captain John Green to West Africa on a ship called *Elizabeth*. Green and Fly began to argue about the pay and Green's brutal punishments. Fly led a mutiny.

> # TIRED OF YOUR CAPTAIN? MUTINY IS THE ONLY WAY. CAPTURE HIM AND GIVE HIM A FAIR TRIAL.
>
> You will find him guilty because you are the judges and jury.
> Send him to swim with the sharks.
> Make your clipper skipper a kipper and send him for a dipper.
> Meet tonight under the main mast. Don't be late.

The men waited till Captain Green lay drunk and asleep. They shook him awake with cries of…

> UP ON DECK, YOU DOG, FOR WE SHALL LOSE NO MORE TIME ABOUT YOU

He was found guilty and the crew invited the captain to choose his own end.

> DO YOU WANT TO JUMP OVERBOARD OR BE TOSSED OVER LIKE A SNEAKING RASCAL?

Hard question. How would YOU answer?

For an hour the captain begged for his life, but the mutineers grew tired of his grovelling and tossed him overboard into the sea to feed the fishes. The captain clung to a trailing rope so one of the mutineers picked up an axe and lopped off his hand.

Fly led the mutiny so he took command of the *Elizabeth*. The crew's first task was to use their sewing skills to make a Jolly Roger flag. Then they renamed the ship *Fame's Revenge*. Sounds more piratical.

They sailed to the east coast of America. They boarded the *John and Betty* and there was one priceless thing on board: a navigator. A clever seaman named William Atkinson knew the North American waters well. Even with Atkinson's help, Fly was a useless captain and a useless pirate. His crew led a mutiny against the mutineer and handed him over to the law to hang.

He showed the hangman how to tie the noose properly then slipped it over his own head. In his last words he moaned about how unfair it all was:

> WE POOR MEN CAN'T GET JUSTICE. THERE'S NO PUNISHMENT FOR OUR CAPTAINS NO MATTER HOW MUCH THEY ABUSE US, AND USE US LIKE DOGS

BLACKBEARD
(c. 1680–1718)

Blackbeard was a man called Edward Teach.

Quick question ... in 1718 the dreaded pirate Blackbeard was shot and beheaded by a navy officer. Blackbeard's body was thrown overboard. What happened next?

Answer: legends say Blackbeard's headless corpse swam round the ship three times before finally sinking.

Blackbeard went into battle with six pistols at his waist and lighted matches under his hat to make him look frightening. (He was a bit of a hot-head.)

The American people became so fed up with Blackbeard they sent a naval ship to stop him. In a hand-to-hand battle Lieutenant Robert Maynard shot Blackbeard dead then cut his head off – just to make sure.

GRÁINNE (c. 1530–1603)

The Pirate Queen Grace O'Malley was born into a family of Irish sailors and traders. She wanted to be a sailor like the rest of her family. But her father told the young girl, 'Your long hair would tangle in the ropes.'

Grace was furious. She dressed like a boy and hacked her hair till it was short as a sailor's. Sorted. She told her father she was ready to sail with him.

LOOK, PA. I'VE GOT A CREW CUT. CREW CUT, GEDDIT?

Her family laughed and gave her a new nickname: Gráinne Mhaol (Grace the Bald). Her father gave in and they set sail for Spain. On the way they were attacked by an English ship. Her father told her to get safely below the decks. Instead, she climbed up a mast. From her perch she spotted an enemy creeping up behind her father with a knife raised.

Grace dropped onto the man's back, kicking, biting and screaming. The terrified man fled and so did the rest of the English attackers. She had saved her father's life.

In 1593 her sons were arrested as rebels when they fought against English rule. Grace went to London to ask Queen Elizabeth I for their release. The two women were nearly the same age – about sixty – when they met at Greenwich Palace.

Grace wore a fine gown, but had a hidden dagger. Guards found it before she could attack the queen. Grace said she only had the dagger to defend herself. Queen Elizabeth believed her.

Grace refused to bow down to Elizabeth because, she said, Elizabeth wasn't the queen of Ireland. Still, Elizabeth liked Grace O'Malley and they reached an agreement:

Both women died in the year 1603.

THE WORST HIGHWAY ROBBERS IN THE WORLD

STICK 'EM UP

DICK TURPIN (1705–39)

The most famous highwayman is probably Dick Turpin. Highwaymen were sometimes known as 'Gentleman of the Road' because they robbed the rich and gave to the poor.

A famous legend says Turpin rode his horse Black Bess from London to York to avoid capture.

Was he a 'gentleman'? Or a common thief and a bully who deserved to hang? What would Turpin say in his cell as he waited to be hanged?

Common thief. That's me. I robbed anyone I could. I started with cattle theft and smuggling. Then I joined a gang that robbed lonely farmhouses. We just kicked the doors down and tortured the owners to tell us where their money was. I remember one time an old widow was said to have £700 in her farmhouse. Nice old dear — just like my old mum. I remember her well. She refused to tell us where the cash was. I hoisted her over her own kitchen fire till she squealed — and when I say squealed... Then I met the famous highwayman, Tom King. I joined him and robbed people in Epping Forest. He was arrested. I went to his rescue and looked through the window of the room where he was a prisoner. I took my gun and fired at the law officer. Sadly I killed Tom King ... I was never a very good shot. Did I ride from London

to York on Black Bess? You're
'aving a laugh, ain't yer? Nah, I
never done that. I went to York to
escape a horse-stealing charge. I
changed me name to John Palmer.
I'd have got away with it too if
I hadn't made a daft mistake. I
shot a chicken. Yes, you heard
me. A chicken. I blasted it with
me pistol for a larf. The owner
reported me. I was arrested. The
law stuck me in this here prison.
I wrote back to Essex and asked
my brother to help me out. Well, me
brother wouldn't pay the sixpence
postage, so the letter went back to
the post office. Would you believe
it? My old schoolteacher saw it
there, recognized me handwriting
and told them I wasn't John Palmer
— I was really the famous Dick
Turpin. They sent him up to York
to identify me.

Would YOUR teacher betray YOU like that? You'd better check before you shoot a chicken.

But that was Turpin's fate. Not much of a hero after all ... torturing an old woman, shooting chickens, killing his partner. On 7 April 1739, Dick Turpin rode to his execution through the streets of York in an open cart. He bowed to the crowds.

At York racecourse he climbed onto the scaffold and then sat for half an hour chatting to the guards and the executioner. He seemed to get bored; he stood up and, without help, threw himself off the ladder. Turpin's body was then taken back to York and kept in the Blue Boar Inn overnight. In those days a pub often had a room that was used to store bodies.

He was buried THREE times. First in St George's churchyard ... then dug up and buried in a doctor's garden – maybe because the docs wanted to experiment on his corpse – then Turpin's friends stole him back and he ended up in St George's again. The stone can still be seen there.

THUGGEES (1200–1800)

The word 'thug' comes from Indian highwaymen, or 'thuggees', who brought terror to the roads of India 400 years before Turpin.

• The word 'thuggee' means 'hidden' and the thuggees were a secret religion. Their members worshipped Mother Kali, the goddess of destruction.

I THOUGHT THAT WAS MY LITTLE SISTER

• They operated as gangs of highway robbers, tricking their victims by being friendly and then strangling them. They used a yellow silk or cloth scarf, which sounds a cosy way to die.

• The thuggees got away with so many murders for 500 years because they were ordinary villagers most of the time. They looked harmless as they spotted a party of travelling strangers and joined them.

• The thuggees had their own secret code and 'Pass the tobacco' meant 'Strangle him now'. They gave their victims a lovely burial.

• They sacrificed goats to their god Kali so their blood spilled down the temple steps night and day.

• But by 1848 the British conquerors had hunted them down and banned the religion.

JENNIE 'LITTLE BRITCHES' STEPHENS

Jennie was aged just sixteen and from a good family when she met Bill Doolin at a dance. Doolin was a member of an American gang of deadly highway, train and bank robbers known as 'The Wild Bunch'.

Jennie followed Doolin back to the gang's hideout, where she worked in a kitchen and on the farm, doing some cattle rustling from time to time.

In 1894, when most of the gang had been killed or captured and Doolin himself had been shot, his body was searched. A poem was found in his pocket, probably written by Jennie:

> Learn to think, for thoughts are noble, learn, oh learn to think aright,
>   Carry out thoughts in action, then press on with all your might.
>   Live to make life grand and noble, live to make it pure and true,
>   Learn to act your own part bravely, learn to think and learn to do.

With the gang mostly dead, Jennie was trapped in a farmhouse. She jumped from a window and rode to safety.

She was chased by a sheriff, who shot her horse because he didn't want to shoot a woman. After a struggle she was captured, and went to prison for two years. Her fate after her release is unknown.

Not all women were so lucky as Jennie. Ella Watson – alias Cattle Kate – bought and sold stolen cattle. She was hanged by a group of cattle owners in 1889.

Turpin's chicken and Ella's cattle cost them their lives.

THE WORST ASSASSINATIONS IN THE WORLD

DEAD ON TARGET

ARCHDUKE FERDINAND (1863–1914)

Killing an important person is usually called assassination. Some assassinations kill more than just the victim though.

Archduke Ferdinand of Austria was hated in Serbia because the Austrians ruled the country. Seven assassins joined a group called the 'Black Hand Gang' that wanted the Austrians out of Serbia. When Ferdi came to Sarajevo in Bosnia they plotted to kill him.

COULDN'T THEY JUST ASK ME TO LEAVE?

1. The Secret Seven armed themselves with guns and bombs at different parts of the route. Ferdi drove through the city in an open-topped car.

2. Assassin Number 1 failed. Ferdi's car drove past. He did nothing.

3. Assassin Number 2 did better. He threw his bomb into Ferdi's car.

4. Ferdi picked it up and threw it out of the car. The bomb blew up under the following car and injured eight innocent people.

5. Ferdi went to the town hall and made a speech. He was driven past Assassins 3, 4, 5 and 6. And they did ... erm ... nothing.

6. Ferdi headed for the hospital to visit the bomb victims. But his driver took a wrong turning. By an

amazing chance this wrong road brought him straight past Assassin Number 7 ... Gavrilo Princip.

7. Princip jumped onto the open car and fired two shots. They killed Ferdi and his wife.

8. Ferdi's dad, the emperor of Austria, was furious. He wanted revenge against all of Serbia's allies. He wanted war.

The world took sides and the First World War started. Two assassin's bullets started a war that killed 20 million people over four years. Germany and Austria and their friends were defeated. They wanted revenge. So, a Second World War started in 1939 and that killed another 80 million. Two assassin bullets – 80 million dead.

Almost every family in Britain, France, Germany and Russia lost someone. You can go to any town or village and see the names of the dead, carved in stone memorials.

GAO JIANLI (230 BC)

Not every assassin is successful. Chinese emperor Qin Shi Huang had many enemies who wanted to see him dead. The first assassin to try was Jing Ke. He offered Qin Shi Huang two gifts…

I OFFER YOU THIS MAP AND THE HEAD OF AN ENEMY GENERAL

THAT'S SO KIND

Jing Ke had hidden a knife in the rolled-up map and stabbed at Qin Shi Huang but missed. The emperor cut him down.

But the assassin had a friend called Gao Jianli who played music on a zither. He was so good the emperor asked him to play at the palace. The emperor loved the music, but someone shouted out…

> THIS IS GAO JIANLI. IT'S THE ASSASSIN JING KE'S BEST FRIEND. HE HAS TO DIE

Gao Jianli was arrested, but the emperor had a problem. He wanted the music but not the killer. So, he came up with an idea.

> LET HIM LIVE BUT HAVE HIM BLINDED

Gao Jianli had his eyes put out then went on playing for the emperor. Yet he still wanted revenge. He had his zither filled with lead, so it was heavy enough to crush a skull.

Blind Gao was trusted enough to get near to the emperor. That was when he swung the heavy zither at the emperor's head. He missed. After all, he was blind.

He was led away to be executed.

HASAN-I SABBĀH
(1050–1124)

Hasan-i Sabbah was the leader of a religious group. As a leader he could be harsh. One man was accused of murder and another of drinking wine.

Both were executed. Both were Hasan-i Sabbah's own sons. Thanks, Dad.

He had lots of enemies but didn't have a powerful army to fight them. He came up with a crafty idea.

The Christian invaders of the region heard stories about Hasan-i Sabbah's killers. They believed they smoked a drug called 'hashish'. They were 'hashish-ins' or 'assassins'.

The drug drove them wild. They looked forward to dying because Hasan-i promised it was a quick way to heaven. The Pope had promised the same thing to his Christian Crusaders.

THE WORST INVASION IN THE WORLD

I'VE GOT THE AXE FACTOR

TASMANIA (1802)

After captain James Cook discovered Australia, Britain used the island as a place to dump its criminals. No one asked the natives if they wanted these men, women and prison guards.

IF WE ASK THEY MIGHT SAY 'NO'

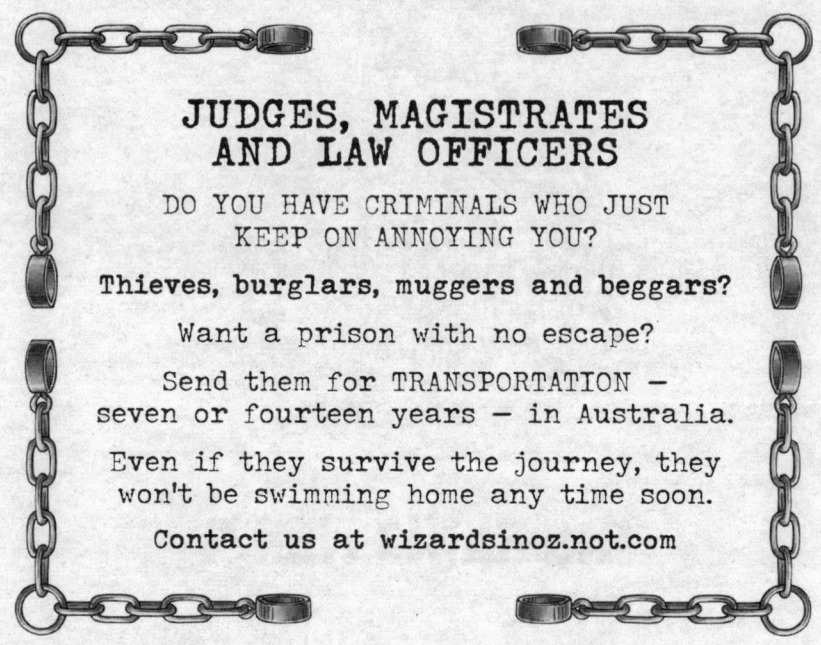

JUDGES, MAGISTRATES AND LAW OFFICERS

DO YOU HAVE CRIMINALS WHO JUST KEEP ON ANNOYING YOU?

Thieves, burglars, muggers and beggars?

Want a prison with no escape?

Send them for TRANSPORTATION — seven or fourteen years — in Australia.

Even if they survive the journey, they won't be swimming home any time soon.

Contact us at wizardsinoz.not.com

The Aboriginal peoples of Tasmania had lived on their island, cut off from Australia, for 12,000 years. They were Stone Age people, but they got along well enough and up to 20,000 lived on the island when the Brits arrived in 1803. Eighty years later there were NONE. Wiped out by convict killers.

These wandering criminals were known as 'Bushrangers' and they brought terror to the native peoples of Tasmania. The bushrangers killed the aboriginals as if they were hunting animals.

Aboriginal men were tied to trees and used for target practice. As one brutal bushranger said...

> I'd shoot an aboriginal as easily as I'd shoot a sparrow. And at the same time, I get a lot of fun from this sort of sport.

The convicts said they had an excuse for being so cruel.

> WE CONVICTS HAVE TRAVELLED HALFWAY ROUND THE WORLD, WATCHING OUR FRIENDS AND FAMILIES DIE ON THE SHIPS; WE ARE FLOGGED AND STARVED. WE HAVE TO BE HARD TO SURVIVE

But it wasn't only the convicts who did this. The people sent to govern the island did it too. Some of the governors of Tasmania – both ladies and gentlemen – hunted aboriginals for 'sport'.

In 1832 a 'kind' British Christian had 220 aboriginals shipped off to Flinders Island, where they could make themselves a new home – except the island was a bleak, cold place. The aboriginals could see their old home, Tasmania, across the water but never return. It's said many died of homesickness.

• More aboriginals died of diseases the British brought and the tribes shrank.

• Settlers spread across the island and the British cattle replaced the aboriginals' kangaroos, so they starved. The tribes shrank again.

• The miserable aboriginals stopped having children – no one really knows why – but that made the tribes die out entirely.

• Some aboriginals began to slaughter their children … babies get in the way when you are fighting to survive. They can give you away by crying.

In 1869 the last native Tasmanian man, King Billy, died of poisoning from drinking too much alcohol.

LINDISFARNE (AD 793)

Historians just cannot agree why the farmers of northern Europe started sailing the world to rob other countries. Were their homelands too crowded? Were the crops too poor? Were they looking for gold or food or land or slaves? Whatever. The farmers became vicious Vikings. One of their first attacks was on a monastery in the north of England in AD 793.

One writer said the monks saw it coming...

> Here were dreadful forewarnings come over the land of Northumbria, and woefully terrified the people: these were amazing sheets of lightning and whirlwinds, and fiery dragons were seen flying in the sky. A great famine soon followed these signs, and shortly after in the same year, on the sixth day before the ides of January, the woeful inroads of heathen men destroyed god's church in Lindisfarne Island by fierce robbery and slaughter.
>
> Anglo-Saxon Chronicle

A strict monk called Alcuin said the wicked monks deserved it. And that he'd warned them.

> Never before has such terror appeared in Britain as we have now suffered from a pagan race. The heathens poured out the blood of saints around the altar and trampled on the bodies of saints in the temple of God, like dung in the streets.
>
> Alcuin, English scholar (AD 735–804)

And that was just the start of nearly 300 years of invasions and terror from Britain to Russia to Rome.

THE AMERICAS (1492)

The Spanish and the Portuguese battled to grab land in South America. Some of the invaders just wanted glory. South America was rich in gold and silver and slaves. Spain and Portugal were Catholic countries, so they asked the Pope to sort out the problem. He said…

> EASILY SETTLED. WE'LL DRAW A LINE DOWN THE MIDDLE OF SOUTH AMERICA, AND SPAIN AND PORTUGAL CAN SHARE IT. DON'T FORGET YOU NEED TO CONVERT THE NATIVES TO BE CHRISTIAN. THEN IT'LL BE FINE TO MAKE THEM SLAVES

The 'conquistadors' from Europe set off with a mission they summed up as…

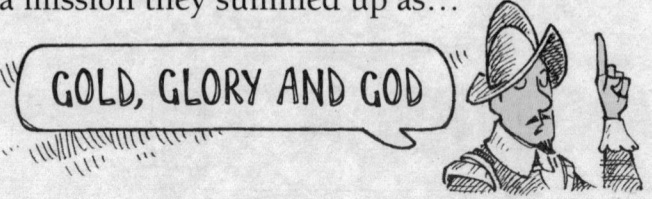

All the conquistadors had to do was read out a new law before they attacked a native enemy. It said…

As usual, no one asked the indigenous peoples of America what they thought. And (as usual) they suffered terribly. In 1492 there were 50 million indigenous Americans. One hundred and fifty years later there were just eight million.

THE WORST SCHOOL IN THE WORLD

EVEN WORSE THAN YOURS

BOWES ACADEMY (1823)

In 1838 Charles Dickens visited Bowes, in County Durham, England. He had heard the stories of William Shaw, the world's worst teacher, who ran the school. He turned the true story of William Shaw into the monster Wackford Squeers in his book *Nicholas Nickleby*. The pupils in his book were...

> ... pale and haggard, with lank and bony bodies, children with the faces of old men, boys of stunted growth and others whose long skinny legs could hardly bear the

> weight of their stooping bodies. All crowded together, were the dull-eye, the hare-lip, the crooked foot and every ugliness of cruelty and neglect. What a growing Hell was breeding here.

But the TRUE story of Bowes School may have been even worse. Just fifteen years before Dickens visited Bowes, the head of the school was taken to court. Parents had paid £20 a year to send their boys there. They were promised good teaching, feeding and bedrooms. Now they said Shaw had neglected their children.

TWO PUPILS BECAME BLIND BECAUSE OF BEATINGS AND POOR FOOD. WHAT CAN YOU SAY ABOUT WHAT YOU SAW?

WE HAD MEAT THREE TIMES A WEEK THAT WAS CRAWLING WITH MAGGOTS, AND BREAD AND CHEESE THE REST OF THE TIME. WE HAD NO SUPPER EXCEPT WARM WATER AND MILK AND DRY BREAD FOR TEA. WE ALL HAD TO WASH IN A TROUGH. WE BOYS SLEPT ON STRAW WITH ONE SHEET TO EACH BED FULL OF FLEAS. FOUR OR FIVE BOYS SLEPT TOGETHER. BOYS WERE BRUTALLY THRASHED

Ten children had gone blind at the school as a result of poor food and cruel punishments. It was common for one pupil to die at Bowes School every year.

Dickens saw the graveyard where the schoolboys were buried. He found the grave of George Ashton Taylor who became 'Smike' for his novel. When he wrote about it the world was shocked. But Dickens blamed the parents who sent their children to places like Bowes. He said…

> Yorkshire schoolmasters are dealers in the greed, heartlessness and stupidity of parents of these helpless children; the teachers are ignorant, dirty, cruel men. Most of us would not trust them to look after our dogs.

In another book, *Hard Times*, Dickens said most of the teaching was useless. Instead of learning things that would help the children in life, they were just taught stuff that would get them through their exams. 'Mr Gradgrind' said…

Nonsense, of course. Nowadays schools would never just teach 'facts' ... except for poor pupils who have to take SATs and GCSE exams.

BIRMINGHAM GIRLS' SCHOOL (1920)

Children were struck on the hand or the backside with a cane ever since schools began in ancient Egypt. It wasn't banned in Britain until the 1980s.

Caning was usually carried out in front of the whole class so everyone could see what happened to wicked children. Then the punishment was written down in a punishment book. We can see what crimes the kids had done.

Which of THESE have YOU done in class?

And which would have earned you the cane back in 1920 at Birmingham Girls' School?

```
• Deliberately disobeying a teacher
• Going into the boys' playground
• Lateness
• Smiling after a teacher told
  her off
• Laziness
• 'Naughty talk' out of school
• Writing in the lavatory
• Talking in class
• Bullying
• Losing a book
```

Answer: ALL of them got a girl the cane at some time in that school. Sometimes a second teacher had to be called in to hold the terrified girl.

TUDOR SCHOOL

Tudor schools were hard work. It was against the school rules to carry a dagger into school – and that rule must have saved a few teachers' lives. The writer Henry Peacham told the tale of a terrible teacher:

On a cold winter morning I know of one teacher who would whip his boys for no reason except to warm himself up. Another beat them for swearing and as he beat them, he swore himself with horrible oaths.

Teachers liked to use 'The Birch' on the backsides of the boys. This was made of thin twigs from a birch tree in a bundle. But one Tudor school had a bit of revenge when a teacher smashed his birch whip on a boy. He told the boys to wait while he went to a birch at the bottom of the school garden to cut a new one.

The thinnest twigs were on the end of the branch that hung over a river. The teacher crawled further and further out to get the thinnest.

Then the branch snapped, and the teacher fell into the river. He drowned.

THE WORST WEAPON IN THE WORLD

THE ATOMIC BOMB (1945)

On 8 May 1945 the Second World War had ended in Europe. Adolf Hitler, the Nazi leader of Germany, had shot himself. His armies gave up the six-year fight, and the troops from Russia, France, USA and Britain had entered Germany.

But over in the East, Japan refused to give up their fight. What the US decided to do was hit the Japanese with a mighty weapon. It would destroy so much the Japanese leader would say, 'We can't fight a force like that. Let's surrender and save Japanese lives.'

That mighty weapon was the atomic bomb. Two were dropped on Japanese cities on 6 and 9 August 1945.

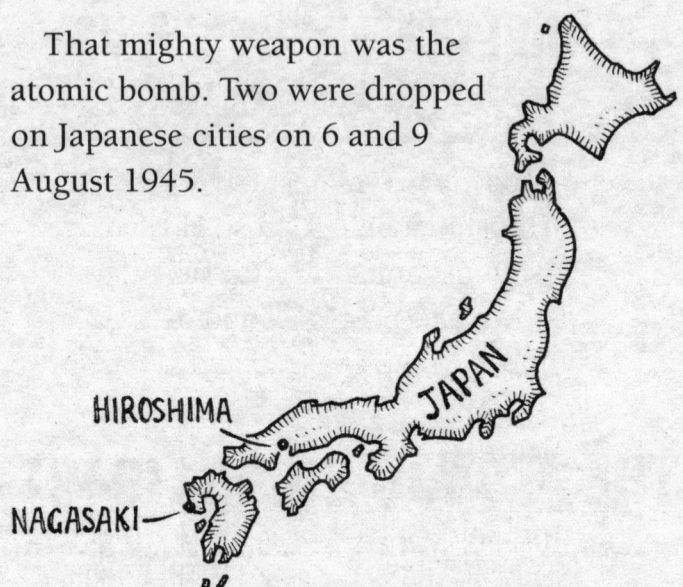

The first bomb, called 'Little Boy', fell on Hiroshima. The Japanese prime minister said Japan would fight on. Three days later 'Fat Man' was dropped on Nagasaki. On 15 August the Japanese gave up.

But it was too late for over 100,000 people. Half were killed in the massive blast of the bombs. The rest died gradually from burns, radiation sickness, and injuries, illness and starvation.

Most of the victims were not fighters – they were ordinary men, women and children.

DID YOU KNOW...?

Tsutomu Yamaguchi was burned by the first bomb on Hiroshima on 6 August. He managed to get home to his hometown the next day. But that hometown was Nagasaki, and on 9 August he was bombed again. He lived and is the only person to survive TWO atomic bombs. He died in 2010 at the age of ninety-three.

The weapons were so terrifying they have never been used since.

THE ANTI-TANK DOG
(1940S)

The Russian army was being attacked by German tanks. The Russian bullets and shells just bounced off the German tank armour.

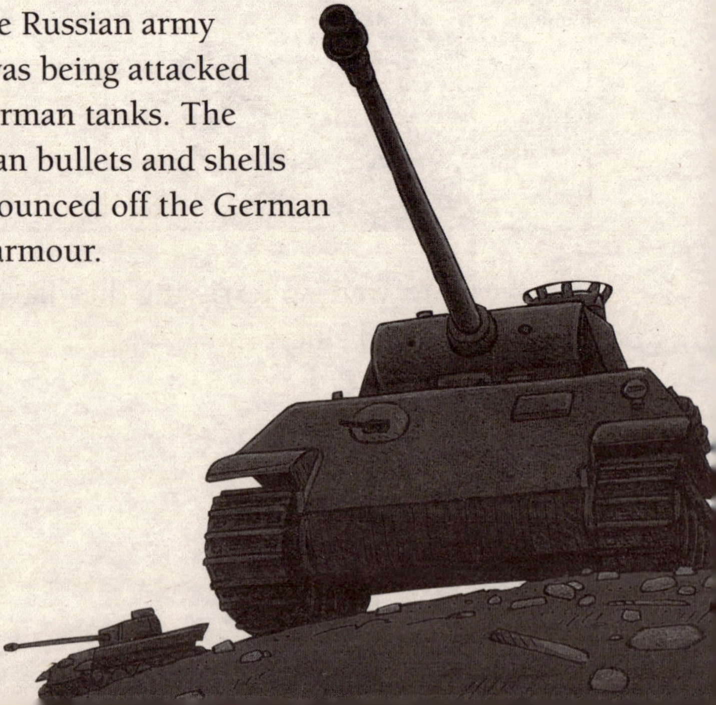

Then a rotten Russian came up with a thought…

That's when the scientists came up with a brilliant but evil plan.

Of course, the dog in a thousand pieces won't feel a thing. Cruel and brilliant BUT…

The Russians used their own T-34 tanks to train the dogs. They put treats under the tanks. But the T-34s had diesel engines.

The German tanks used petrol and smelled different to Russian tanks. The battle came and the mutts followed their noses.

The dogs ran under the diesel tanks – the Russian tanks. You do NOT get a prize for guessing what happened next.

THE CIRCULAR WARSHIP (1877)

In the 1877 war between Russia and Turkey the Russians launched an iron warship, the *Novgorod*.

It was as round as a floating soup dish.

It had six steam engines that drove six propellors. It had large cannon and was sent off to blast the towns on the enemy coast.

But when a gun was fired, it sent *Novgorod* into a spin.

It was useless. But it was no worse than some of the other weapons of war invented down the ages...

• Bat bombs: US bats were to be released over Japanese cities. They'd roost on the wooden and paper houses. A timer would set off a firebomb that was fastened to the bat, ruin the house and kill the bat. The bat bomb was tested in the USA and burned down part of the army test base. It was never used against a Japanese city. A batty idea.

- The iron hand: invented by the brilliant Archimedes in 213 BC. It was a giant claw. When the Romans attacked Archimedes' home city his claw would swoop down on the Roman ships, pick them up and drop them back to smash. It was never used. Battier than a bat.

- The Pykrete battleship: this was a British battleship made from a material invented by Geoffrey Pyke in 1943. Pykrete was made from sawdust frozen in ice. Tougher than steel and very slow to melt. Never made. Battier than a flock of vampire bats.

EPILOGUE

But that's human beings for you. Someone comes up with something bad, then someone else comes up with something worse. Just when you think it can't get any worse, along comes the worst.

The worst in the world.

You've read thirty of the *Horrible Histories* 'worsts'. One thing is certain: NO ONE WILL AGREE with them all.

INTERESTING INDEX

Where will you find pirates and pandemics, volcanoes and Vikings, death and disasters, and meteorites and mudlarks in an index? In a Horrible Histories book, of course!

Aboriginal peoples 250-2
Alexander the Great 65-7, 69
Amina (Nigerian queen) 158-9
Amundsen, Roald (explorer) 178, 179
Antarctic 178-9
Archimedes (Greek inventor) 275
assassinations 240-7
Athens plague 127-8
atomic bomb 267-9
Aztecs 130-2

bat bombs 274

Bathory, Countess Elizabeth (serial killer) 155-7
battles 40-50
Becket, Thomas (archbishop) 119-20
Birmingham Girls' School 262-3
Black Death (plague) 122-4, 216
Black Douglas (knight) 113-15
Blackbeard (pirate) 225-6
blood, bathing in 156-7
Borgia, Lucrezia (alleged poisoner) 160-2
Bosworth, Battle of 48-50
Bowes Academy, Country Durham 258-61

Buckingham Palace 106-8

caning (children) 262, 263, 265
cannon, death by 91
Carthage 52-3
castles 197-204
Cathars 116-18
Catholics and Protestants 116-18, 136-7, 190-4, 214-15
Changping, Battle of 41-4
cholera 37-9
Colosseum, Rome 87-8
Columbus, Christopher (explorer) 33, 147-9
conquistadors (soldier-explorers) 255-6
convict killers 249-50
Cook, Captain James (explorer) 176-7, 240
Cotswold Olympics 25-7
Cromwell, Oliver (Puritan leader) 136-7
Crusades 120, 133-5
Curse of Cromwell (Irish massacre) 136-7

Dickens, Charles 258, 260
diseases 9-10, 30-9, 82, 122-8, 168, 169-70
    weird cures 138-45
dogs, anti-tank 270-2
Drake, Sir Francis 151

Eastland, SS (ship) SS 54-5
Elagabalus (Roman emperor) 16, 95-7
Elizabeth I (queen of England) 33, 34, 150-1, 190-1, 228-9
emperors 15-17, 59-67, 95-7, 216, 244-5

famine 80-2
Fawkes, Guy 93, 190, 192
Ferdinand, Archduke of Austria 241-3

First World War 125, 217-18, 243
Fly, William (pirate) 222-4
food 11-19, 96, 165
French Revolution 72-3

Gao Jianli (would-be assassin) 244-5
George IV (king of England) 106
George VI (king of England) 108
Georgian cures 142-3
ghosts 198-9, 200, 201-2
gladiators 70, 86, 88
Grace O'Malley (pirate queen) 227-9
Groom of the Stool (toilet attendant) 164-6
Gugasian, Carl (robber) 211-12
guillotine 73
Gunpowder Plot 92-3

Haiti slave revolt 74-5
hanging, drawing and quartering 93
Hasan Sabah (religious leader) 246-7
Hastings, Battle of 45-7
Henry I (king of England) 119-20
Henry VIII (king of England) 164-6, 185-6
highway robbers 230-9
Hiroshima 268-9
Holy Roman Empire 214-16
Hopkins, Matthew (witch finder) 195-6
human sacrifice 96, 130-2
Hylton Castle 198-9

Incas 139-41
Indian Mutiny 89-91
Indigenous Americans 147-9, 255-6
invasions 248-56
Irene of Athens (empress) 63-4
Irish famine 80-2

iron hand (weapon) 275
Ivan the Terrible (Russian ruler) 181-4

jobs 163-70
journeys 171-9
Julius Caesar of Austria 100-1

Kelly, Ned (outlaw) 209-10
knights 112-20

Leap Castle 201-2
leprosy 35-6
lifeboats 55
Louis XIV (king of France: 'Sun King') 109, 110
Louis XVI (king of France) 73, 110-11

Magellan, Ferdinand (explorer) 172-5
Marie Antoinette (French queen) 73
matches, making 169-70
meteorite 83-4
Moosham Castle 203-4
Morro Castle (ship) 56-8
mudlarks (scavengers) 167-8
Murad IV (Turkish sultan) 98-9
mutineers 173, 222-4

Nagasaki 268, 269
natural disasters 76-84

Oates, Lawrence (explorer) 179
Olympic sports 20-9

palaces 102-11
pandemics 121-8
pankration (wrestling) 22-4
Paris Commune 18-19

Peasants' Revolt 104-5
Pericles (Athenian leader) 128
Philip II (Macedonian king) 65-6
phossy jaw (disease) 169-70
pigeon shooting 29
pirates 221-9
plagues 10, 122-4, 127-8
    weird cures 144-5
poisoning 160
Pompeii 77-9
poo and sewage 166, 167-8
Punic Wars 52-3
punishments 71, 85-93, 96, 97, 117, 134, 149, 153, 182, 183, 204, 262-3, 264-5
    torturers 189-96
Pykrete battleship 275

Qin Shi Huang (Chinese emperor) 244-5

rebellions 68-75, 104-5
religions 129-37
    see also Catholics and Protestants
Richard III (king of England) 48-9
robbers 205-12, 230-9
Roman Games 86-8
Romans 15-17, 52-3, 69-71, 77-9, 86-8, 95-7, 152-3, 275
rulers 180-8
    see also emperors

schools 257-65
Scott, Captain Robert (explorer) 178-9
scurvy 9, 174
sea disasters 51-8
Second World War 108, 267, 270-2
Shaka (Zulu chief) 187-8

Shaw, William (teacher) 258-61
shin-kicking 26-7
Simon de Montfort (nobleman) 116-18
slaves
    punishments 71, 153
    rebellions 69-71, 74-5
    slavers 146-53
smallpox 31-4
Spanish flu 125-6
Sparta 127-8
Spartacus 69-71
Stephens, Jennie (robber) 237-9
Stone Age food 12-14

Taillefer (jester) 46-7
Tasmania 249-52
Thirty Years' War 214-16
thuggees (highway robbers) 235-6
Timur/Tamburlaine (warlord) 219-20
Titanic (ship) 54-5, 56, 179
toilets 110, 166
Torquemada, Thomas (monk) 193-4
Toussaint L'Ouverture (slave leader) 75
Tower of London 103-5
Tudor schools 264-5
Turpin, Dick (highwayman) 231-4
Twm Siôn Cati (robber) 206-8

typhus 82

Versailles 109-11
Vesuvius (volcano) 77-9
Vibi Perpetua (Christian martyr) 87-8
Victoria (queen of England) 107
Viking invasions 253-4

Waad, William (torturer) 190-2
wars 52-3, 108, 125, 127-8, 133-7, 213-20, 243, 267
warship, circular 273-4
Watson, Ella (robber) 239
weapons 266-75
werewolves 204
Wild Bunch (robbers) 237-8
William the Conqueror 45, 47, 103, 106
William de Tracy (knight) 119-20
Windsor Castle 106
witches 195-6, 203-4
women, worst 154-62

youths, worst 94-101

Zheng (Chinese emperor) 60-1
zoo animals, eating 19

TERRY DEARY

Terry Deary was born at a very early age, so long ago he can't remember. But his mother, who was there at the time, says he was born in Sunderland, north-east England, in 1946 – so it's not true that he writes all *Horrible Histories* from memory. At school he was a horrible child only interested in playing football and giving teachers a hard time. His history lessons were so boring and so badly taught, that he learned to loathe the subject. *Horrible Histories* is his revenge.

MARTIN BROWN

Martin Brown was born in Melbourne, on the proper side of the world. Ever since he can remember he's been drawing. His dad used to bring back huge sheets of paper from work and Martin would fill them with doodles and little figures. Then, quite suddenly, with food and water, he grew up, moved to the UK and found work doing what he's always wanted to do: drawing doodles and little figures.

COLLECT THEM ALL!

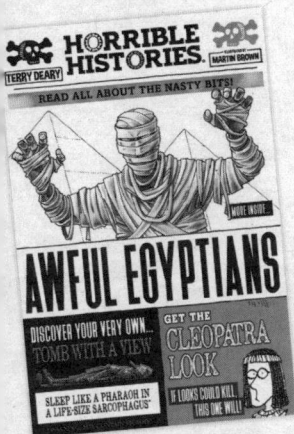

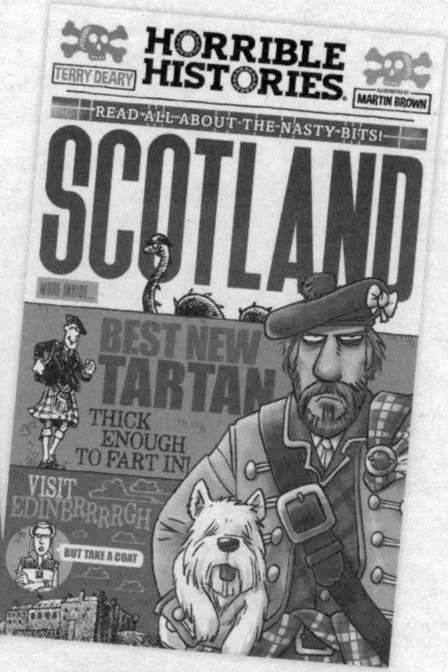